Cheers!

LONDON & NEW YORK

A SPIRITED GUIDE TO Liquors and LIQUEURS

DISTILLED, BLENDED AND BOTTLED BY

FRANCESCA WHITE
180° PROOF

PADDINGTON PRESS LTD
NEW YORK & LONDON

Library of Congress Cataloging in Publication Data

White, Francesca, 1940–
    Cheers!: A spirited guide to liquors and liqueurs.

    Includes indexes.
    1. Liquors. 2. Liqueurs. I. Title.
TP597.W45   641.2′5   76-53321
ISBN 0-448-23165-4

Copyright © 1977 Paddington Press Ltd.
All rights reserved
Filmset and printed in England by BAS Printers Limited,
Wallop, Hampshire
Bound by Garden City Press Ltd., London &
Letchworth
Designed by Richard Johnson
Cover illustration by David Bull
Illustrations by Jeremy Blezzard
Maps and diagrams by Patricia Pillay

IN THE UNITED STATES
PADDINGTON PRESS LTD.
Distributed by
GROSSET & DUNLAP

IN THE UNITED KINGDOM
PADDINGTON PRESS LTD.

IN CANADA
Distributed by
RANDOM HOUSE OF CANADA LTD.

IN AUSTRALIA
Distributed by
ANGUS & ROBERTSON PTY. LTD.

Ingredients

A Note on the Recipe Sections and Bar Equipment

Tʜɪs book is about distilled spirits: liquors and liqueurs. It is written for all drinkers, to promote their interest in the story, composition, manufacture and diversity of the various spirits, in the hope that they will all the more relish the taste—and tradition—of what they drink.

At the end of each chapter on the individual spirits I have listed a number of classic recipes for cocktails and mixed drinks. The measurements are in parts—for instance, 2 parts spirit to 1 part fruit juice—so that you can use whatever type of measure you prefer, whether it be a jigger (1½ liquid oz.), a pony (1 liquid oz.), or just a slug (although this is not recommended).

To equip a home bar a few simple good pieces of equipment are necessary. Besides the basic measuring cup of your choice you will need a cocktail shaker, a mixing

glass with a beaker (for drinks which include wines and vermouths), a lemon squeezer, a large ice bucket, and a variety of stemmed cocktail glasses, tumblers and tall glasses with a few mugs for hot drinks.

Besides your stock of spirits and liqueurs you will also need a gomme (which you can either buy, or make at home by boiling sugar and water to be used in the same measurements as you would solid sugar) or grenadine, a pomegranate-flavored syrup which gives a nice tinge to your cocktail; Angostura bitters and/or orange bitters; and the usual mixers (soda water, tonic water, ginger ale, etc.).

Recipes calling for shaking in a cocktail shaker need plenty of ice to shake over. Do not make more cocktails than are needed for one round, as watery fill-ups are horrible. Fresh fruit juices should be used unless stated otherwise.

The Drink Story

WHY do people drink? Is it because they like the taste of alcohol, or because they like its effects? Certainly the latter reason plays the dominant role in the history of drinking. Primitive wines and beers, not to mention the first distilled spirits (which were invented somewhat later in the game), tasted so ghastly that they had to be heavily spiced and sweetened to disguise the crude flavor of the alcohol. And yet men preferred alcohol to the sweet juice of the grape, and continued to favor it long after governments as early as Hammurabi's in the second millennium BC recognized it as a God-sent source of revenue and began taxing it up to the stars. Certainly, it was not the taste people were after, but the pleasing afterglow.

The euphoric effect of alcohol is a paradox, for contrary to common supposition alcohol is a depressant, not a stimulant. It acts upon the brain, and slows down that part of it which controls our judgment and behavior, our social inhibitions. Under its influence we become less hesitant, less self-critical, more lively and more effusive. We behave with less restraint, in a more relaxed fashion.

This feeling of relaxation and well-being fosters conviviality and good-will, and for this reason alcohol has played a vital role in so many diferent societies. But like all depressants and drugs, when taken in excess it can be harmful—even poisonous at times. The immediate effect of overindulgence is that we become intoxicated. That part of the brain which controls reflex actions and muscular movements is impaired: man staggers, he slurs his words, he becomes stupefied. He is drunk.

What is society's reaction to this? For the most part, the ancient and classical world tolerated it as a natural occurrence: they encouraged ritual intoxication in religious ceremonies and condoned it in private life. Some condemned it in public figures, but on the whole drunkenness was a fact of life. Not so among the Hebrews, though. They viewed drunkenness, whether public or private, as overindulgence and strictly condemned it on moral grounds. This attitude was subsequently adopted by the whole of Christendom: wine is a gift of God, but excessive indulgence is a sin.

But sinful or not, people still got drunk, and with the advent of spirits drunkenness became such a dreadful social evil that governments were forced to take some action. In London, during the terrible Gin Era in the 1700s, the government tripled taxation on spirits to curb drunkenness. So be it, but they only succeeded in encouraging illicit distillation, which is exactly what happened in America when the government tried to enforce Prohibition. History seems to support the ancient Chinese sage who maintained that no law will ever be successful in enforcing men to abstain from drink. What governments, and still more dedicated social reformers, have succeeded in doing is to attack some of the root causes of overindulgence: poverty, lack of alternative leisure activities and mental stress.

Let us take a look at the drink story and see how man has used alcohol, and indeed abused it, throughout history. Although this is a book about distilled alcohol—that is, liquors and liqueurs, rather than wines and beers—it is necessary to begin our study with wine and beer as these were the earliest forms of alcohol known to man. Indeed, spirits did not impinge on his history, in the Western world at any rate, till he was well into the middle age of his life on earth, whereas wine and beer accompanied his infancy and adolescence. And truly they watered the very roots of his civilization.

DRINK AND MYTHOLOGY

The origin of alcohol goes back at least two million years ago when man most probably chanced upon it accidentally and found it to his liking. The sap in a hollow branch if left all day would naturally ferment, and by evening would produce a feeling of happiness and well-being in those who drank of it.

Drink, once discovered, was treasured. It was looked upon as a gift of the gods, a gift which in turn man offered back to the deity in his sacrificial rites. Together with other precious stuffs it was the tribute paid to kings. Together with food it was the gift of hospitality—as it is today. It became an important part of man's daily diet and a necessity of life, giving strength and health.

In most mythologies the gods drink and feast. An early account of celestial conviviality is given in the Babylonian *Epic of Creation* written about 2225 BC. The gods drink and:

> sweet drink put far away their cares. As they drank liquor their bodies became satiated. Much they bubbled and their mood was exalted.

In Homer, too, the gods are frequently in their cups.

Ganymede and Hebe are their two special cupbearers, whose sole function is to keep the cups filled. Often the gods have recourse to drink before battle. In the *Rgveda*, the Brahmin poems collected about 1500 BC, the great god Indra always takes inebriating liquor before tackling his archenemy Vrtra.

Among mortals it was a woman who first discovered alcohol. According to a Persian legend, a mythological king called Jamshid one day opened a jar in which his grapes were stored and found instead a strong-smelling, purplish liquid. He had the jar labeled "poison" and returned it to his cellars. It happened that a courtesan, weary of her lonely and neglected state, came across the jar and decided to end her life. She drank, she slept, and then she awoke feeling light of heart. She hastened to the king and told him of her discovery, and from that day on many jars of grapes were left to ferment and the precious result was served to royal guests.

According to another legend, this time from Mesopotamia, it was again a woman who introduced drink to primitive man. Gilgamesh, an epic hero of the third millennium BC, was a wicked tyrant. So the gods, moved by the prayers of the people, created a savage hero Enkidu who was to overcome Gilgamesh. A *hetaera*, a young serving girl, approached this wild man of the woods and taught him for the first time the joys of civilization.

> He in the past of the milk of wild things
>   to suck was accustomed,
> Bread which she set before him he broke,
>   but gazed and stared,
> Enkidu bread did not know how to eat,
>   nor had he knowledge
> Mead how to quaff.

DRINK AND THE PRE-CLASSICAL WORLD

Drink was the prime offering to the gods in ancient rituals. In the *Zend Avesta*, the sacred book of the Zoroastrians, directions are given for the preparation of *haoma*, an intoxicating liquor for the sacrificial rite. The offering of the Vedic sacrifice was *soma*, the juice of a plant extracted by pressing the stalks between stones. The juice was then filtered through sheep's wool and mixed with water or milk. The Jews burned wine upon their altars, while from the earliest known anthology of Chinese poetry, the *Shih Ching*, compiled at the time of Confucius in about the sixth

TOP: *A king offers wine before a Sphinx, the emblem of royal dignity.*
BOTTOM: *King Sety the First offers wine before the gods Osiris, Isis and their son Horus.*

13

century BC, we learn that the Chinese offered their spirits to the gods in thanksgiving for a good harvest:

Now when our barns are filled with grain
    And myriad stacks in fields remain
Spirits and viands we prepare
    To use on grand occasion rare
In sacrificial rite.

The Egyptians offered drink to their great god Osiris and to their lesser gods, and left it in tombs with other precious possessions for their dead. They offered wine to their gods rather than beer, as this was considered an inferior drink. In the production of wine they were highly skilled. The vines were grown in cordons not very high from the ground, whereas the vines for table fruit were grown in the leisure gardens on trellises and pergolas. The harvesting was done by kneeling men and the grapes were either trodden by men holding onto ropes to support them, or pressed and mashed by a laborer twisting a sack of

grapes till the juice poured out. The strength of the man holding the two poles apart must have been considerable. Wine was stored in jars, which were then labeled and their mouths covered with conical caps of mud on which seals were stamped.

Libations were poured out to the gods as a preliminary ceremony in all sacrifices. They were also consumed, in varying degrees of moderation, by the priests and sacrificers. Among the more temperate were the followers of Zoroaster and the Jewish priests, who were forbidden to drink before performing their duties; during the sacrifice, though, they did partake of small quantities. Not so the Brahmins, who drank freely and considered intoxication a vital part of their ritual. The hymns of the *Rgveda* are full of exhortations like:

> Called by us, O Indra, sit down and intoxicate thyself with us, thy friends.

Man also used alcohol as a tribute to his king. The *Shih Ching* tells how part of the "good spirits" which were not used in sacrifices were taken to the ruler and there drunk in handsome rhinocerous horns as a toast to his good health:

> *In the ninth month the cold begins with frost :*
> *the tenth their cornyards swept and clean they boast.*
> *Good spirits in two vessels kept they take*
> *to help their joy, and this proposal make :*
> *We'll kill both lambs and sheep they joyous say*
> *and to the Ruler quickly take our way.*
> *We'll mount his hall ; the massive cup we'll raise*
> *made of rhinocerous horn ; and as we praise*
> *wish him long life, the life of endless days.*

In Egypt, too, wine was a common tribute to the ruler, and also exchanged between royalty as a precious gift.

Lastly, alcoholic beverages were used freely as a token of hospitality. Again the *Shih Ching* describes how the lesser lords received their guests and offered them drink in more homely cups:

> *Dried gourds for cups are with the spirit filled*
> *so does the duke his friends and chieftains feast.*

Ordinary folk also got their families together over a drink:

> *I've strained and made my spirits clear*
> *the fatted lamb I've killed;*
> *with friends who my own surname bear*
> *my hall I've largely filled.*

DRINKS OF THE WORLD

The Assyrians and the Hittites pledged one another in wine, filling their wine cups from the mixing bowl. Banquets are frequently depicted in Egyptian paintings, where serving girls as well as guests wear garlands of flowers while yet more flowers decorate the wine jars and the cups. Sometimes these were of glass, more often of glazed pottery. Fish were often painted on the concave inside surface of the cup, so that when it was filled the fish seemed to be swimming in the liquid.

THE BRITISH LIBRARY

THE BRITISH LIBRARY

In antiquity drink was made to aid man in his religious, civil and social activities. But with drink there also came abuse of it. As far back as the year 2000 BC it was found necessary to restrict the use of alcohol and enforce laws regarding its sale.

Different societies reacted differently to drunkenness. In antiquity the prevalent attitude was one of tolerance of individual folly, yet condemnation of it in a public figure such as a priest or ruler. But this is not always the case: the Greek historian Herodotus recounts the following custom current among the Persians:

> If an important decision is to be made, they discuss the question when they are drunk, and the following day the master of the house where the decision was held submits their decision for reconsideration when they are sober. If they still approve it, it is adopted; if not, it is abandoned. Conversely any decision they make when they are sober is reconsidered afterwards when they are drunk.

Drunkenness had another special function among the ancients: it was frequently used as a means of overcoming one's enemies. Jupiter slew his father Kronos after he had made him drunk. Ra, the Egyptian god, poured beer over the whole world in order to inebriate the monster cow Hathor, who was systematically slaughtering mankind. Odysseus made the Cyclops drunk and thus escaped from his clutches. The Hebrew maiden Judith made the enemy general Holofernes drunk in his tent, cut off his head and thus saved her people. Cyrus made war upon Tomyris,

queen of the Massagetae. As a ruse he pretended to abandon his camp, leaving behind him flowing goblets of wine. The enemy invaded the camp, drank the wine and fell asleep. Cyrus then overcame them in their stupor and marched them off as his prisoners.

Of all the ancient peoples the Hebrews were the most severe in their reprimand of drunkenness, as the Bible clearly states, whether the offender be an ordinary citizen or a public figure. Indeed, the Hebrews did drink wine on occasions of hospitality and at public festivals. They drank it at circumcisions, at weddings, and to toast the soul of the departed; and wine was used as an accompaniment to the prayers celebrating both the beginning and the end of the Sabbath. But the purpose of drinking was clearly in reverence of an occasion, and overindulgence leading to drunkenness was socially unacceptable.

Temperance writers of the nineteenth and twentieth centuries have gone a bit out of their way to capitalize on the ancient Hebrews' attitude toward overindulgence, and ever since the great temperance movements of the last century there has been a controversy over the scriptural doctrine on drink and drinking.

In Hebrew there are two words for the juice of the grape: *tirosh*, denoting the unfermented must; and *yayin*, denoting fermented must, i.e. wine. Temperance writers maintain that the Old Testament permits the drinking of *tirosh* but not of *yayin*. The sense of the Scriptures, however, often depends on the context of the passage as much as on the precise meaning of the words. For example, in Micah VI:15, it is stated that:

Thou shalt sow, but thou shalt not reap :
Thou shalt tread the olives, but thou
shalt not anoint thee with oil :
and sweet must [tirosh]*, but thou shalt*
not drink wine [yayin]*.*

Temperance writers construe this as an injunction, whereas the sense of the whole passage seems to be a curse, God's withholding from the Jews of the *good* things of life—bread, oil and wine—on account of a specific act of disobedience.

DRINK IN THE CLASSICAL WORLD

On the whole, the Greeks and Romans adopted the same attitudes as the ancient civilizations concerning the use and abuse of alcohol. Wine in the form of an offering and a libation was an essential part of Greek religious festivals, especially among the Maenads, the female worshippers of Dionysus, their god of wine. Drink together with food was offered as a show of hospitality and wine flowed freely at convivial gatherings. Drunkenness was mildly ridiculed in the individual and frowned upon in the ruler or general. Homer had his Trojan hero Hector refuse wine from his mother prior to embarking upon his sacred duty as a warrior:

Bring me no honey-hearted wine, my lady mother, lest thou cripple me of my courage and I be forgetful of my might.

But the social drinking customs of the Greeks differ from those of the Egyptians. At their feasts both men and women were present, albeit often at different ends of the room. The Greek symposium was for men only. It took place after dinner when the tables had been cleared and a libation had been poured to the gods. Then a hymn of thanksgiving was sung and the drinking commenced, the gathering being enlivened by dancing girls, flute players and other musicians. Wine was what they drank, mixed with water. The Greeks were well known for the sparseness of their eating and drinking habits. They considered drinking undiluted wine as fit only for barbarians. In general their gatherings were temperate and followed the counsel of their poet Eubulus:

Three bowls only do I mix for the temperate:
one to health, which they empty first,
the second to love and pleasure,
the third to sleep. When this is drunk up
the wise guests go home.

But not always was this counsel followed: to cite one very well-known example, the guests described in Plato's *Symposium*, including the great philosopher Socrates, all had distinct hangovers from the night before.

The Greeks drank in the evening, after the day and its various tasks had drawn to an end:

Drink! Why wait for lamps? The day
Has not another inch to fall.
Fetch the biggest beakers—they
Hang on pegs along the wall.

These beakers were usually in the form of a cyclix, a shallow two-handled bowl into which the wine and water were ladled from the mixing bowl.

The Greeks also drank in their taverns, which were frequently houses of ill-repute, sometimes providing theatrical entertainments for their guests.

In Rome, too, taverns abounded. At Pompeii, 118 *popinas*, or bars, have been identified, each block of houses having its own. Outside the tavern a bush or a garland of leaves was hung to indicate that wine was being served within. This custom persisted well into the Middle Ages and gave rise to the saying "Good wine needs no bush."

As with the Greeks wine was to become the common drink of the Romans, but in the early years following the foundations of Rome, the beverage was downright scarce. So scarce, in fact, that King Numa forbade the sprinkling of wine on funeral pyres and ordered that milk, not wine, be offered in sacrifice to the gods. And so strong was the concern that wine not be wasted, that one is led to wonder if it was out of regard for their virtue alone that women were forbidden to drink wine at this time. Punishment for offenders tended to be rather severe: the historian Pliny tells of several women being slain by their husbands or starved to death by their relations for stealing the precious liquid.

By the second century BC, however, wine had become the common beverage: it was used in religious ceremonies, in trade and commerce, and at banquets, where it was

*Etruscans swilling from conventional
wine containers, a skin and an
amphora.*

DRINKS OF THE WORLD (1892)

drunk to great excess by both men and women. A famous
description of one of these banquets in imperial times is
given by the satirist Petronius in his account of
Trimalchio's feast.

Trimalchio was a self-made man of colossal wealth,
eager to impress his crowd of hangers-on with his newly
acquired opulence. A libation to the gods inaugurates the
meal. Then the hors d'oeuvres are served, followed by
honey wine. Inferior wine is then poured over the guests'
fingers to rinse them and the procession of precious wines
starts. Between each course, one more sumptuous than the
next, *ministratores* replenish the cups of the guests with
every sort of wine. The amphorae are uncorked at the table
and the wine is strained into the mixing bowl from which
the cups are filled. Dinner is followed by the *comissatio*, or
ceremonial drinking match, presided over by the master of
ceremonies whose duty it is to prescribe at the proposal of
each toast how many cups are to be emptied all in one
draught. Trimalchio threatens to pour wine over the head
of any of his guests who are not up to this. As might be
expected, the feast ends in utter debauchery and drunkenness.

Roman historians relate that daily drunkenness was
prevalent not only among the rich, but among the plebs
who spent their days drinking and gambling in the taverns

and indulging in all manner of dissipation. On the other hand, there are the poets who have left us less gross accounts of Roman drinking habits, and have sung most elegantly of the infinite pleasures wine brings to man.

Pour in Callistus two double measures of Falernian,
  Do thou Alcinus dissolve upon them the summer snow
Let my dripping locks be rich with overbounteous balm
  and my temples droop beneath the knotted roses.

As the Roman Empire spread, the Romans encountered new drinks. Among the German tribes they found that beer and mead were the staple drink. The Germans spent much of their time in drinking bouts, and often, like the Persians, discussed matters of state under the influence. They also enjoyed drinking wagers and pledging healths, and were known for their hospitality towards wayfarers and strangers to whom food and drink was always offered. The Teutonic gods reveled at mighty banquets in the halls of the Valhalla, together with the souls of the dead warriors who feast forever, served by the beautiful Valkyries who filled their cups with ale gushing from the udders of the great goat Heidrun.

THE MIDDLE AGES

In Europe during the Middle Ages alcohol continued to be used for pleasure and hospitality. Anglo-Saxon hospitality stretched from lord to humble peasant. Toasts and pledges were their custom when drinking, a toast being so-called because a piece of spiced toast was floated in the cup. The cup was handed to the host who drank and then passed it to his neighbor. When the cup had done the round of the table it was handed back to the host who drained it and ate the toast in honor of his guests.

The custom of pledging someone as you drank developed during the Danish occupation of England in the tenth century AD, when, if an Englishman presumed to drink in the presence of a Dane without express permission, it was esteemed such a great mark of disrespect that he was instantly put to death. The English became so intimidated that they would not drink unless a Dane pledged their safety and stood guard over them as they drank.

As in classical times, the tables were withdrawn after the meal, and the hands of the guests were washed. Then the party commenced drinking. The lord and his chief guests

THE BRITISH LIBRARY

sat on a high seat with their guards and cupbearers at their sides, while the other guests sat around on benches. Among the wealthier classes professional minstrels entertained the guests with their recitations, while among the humbler folk each guest contributed to the festivities. Their drink was ale and mead, the latter being produced in great quantities as can be reckoned from the enormous production of honey recorded by the Normans in their *Domesday Book*, a survey of Anglo-Saxon England.

Mead horns are mentioned in the great Anglo-Saxon epic, *Beowulf*, and are generally said to be made from oxen horns and sometimes ivory. These drinking vessels were at times donated by kings and chieftains as tenure horns, given together with a land gift as proof that the land had indeed been bequeathed. Cups too were left as bequests. The lady Ethilgivia left to the abbey of Ramsey: "two silver cups for the use of the brethren in the refectory, in order that while drink is served in them to the brethren at their repast, my memory may be more firmly imprinted in their hearts."

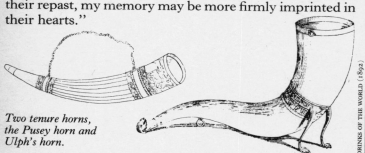

Two tenure horns, the Pusey horn and Ulph's horn.

DRINKS OF THE WORLD (1892)

Fine wines and ale in the Middle Ages were always to be found at the monasteries, where the monks had their own vineyards and did their own brewing. In the monastery of St. Gall during the tenth century each monk received daily five measures of beer besides occasional allowances of wine on feast days. Healths were often pledged by the abbot, and the general intemperance of the clergy is a noted feature throughout medieval history. A German preacher, Rabanus Maurus, inveighs against this failing and prescribes punishments:

If a monk drinks till he vomits, he
must do thirty days' penance;
if a priest or a deacon, forty
days ... if a priest gets drunk
through inadvertence, he
must do penance seven days,
if through carelessness
fifteen days.

An earlier saint had decreed:

> If any monk drinking too freely gets thick of speech,
> so that he cannot join in the psalmody, he is to be
> deprived of his supper.

In the twelfth century the chronicle of St. Edmunds-
bury tells of how the abbot wept at the drunken state of his
congregation, and of how he punished them:

> The rioters were obliged to do penance by stripping
> themselves altogether naked except their drawers, to
> prostrate themselves before the door of the church;
> and when the abbot saw more than a hundred men
> lying down naked, he wept. They were then sharply
> whipped and absolved.

Drunkenness, which was usually tolerated in ancient
societies with the exception of the Hebrews, becomes in
the Middle Ages a punishable offense, both for the clergy
and the laity, on religious and moral grounds. Olaus
Magnus in his history of the northern people of the late
Middle Ages has a long dissertation on the punishment of

drinkers. He first gives an account of the effect of the alcohol on different northern races: the Finns become weepy, and the Germans quarrelsome; the Goths obstreperous and the Gauls petulant. He sums up his treatise with a suggested punishment for drunkards: let them be sat upon a sharp wedge and compelled to down an entire horn of ale, after which let them be hauled up and down upon the wedge by a rope.

Drunkenness in both clergy and laity continued to be punished throughout the following centuries. At the beginning of the seventeenth century a law was passed in England that every drunkard should be fined five shillings and spend six hours in the stocks. Up to the early nineteenth century, church wardens would leave the divine service at the commencement of the second lesson and scour all public houses, putting anyone who was found drinking in the stocks which were conveniently situated by the churchyard. During the Commonwealth a drunkard's coat was devised, consisting of a wooden barrel with a hole at the top, through which the culprit's head was passed, and two slots at the sides for his arms. This punishment, like that of putting drunkards in the stocks to be teased by urchins, continues the tradition of ridiculing drunkenness; which, being such a prevalent vice, society finds difficult to condemn with harsher punishments.

Drunkard's coat designed as a punishment during the Commonwealth in the 1650s.

Drinking in the Middle Ages was done both in the lord's hall and in the peasant's cottage, but also very frequently in the tavern. Inns were often attached to monasteries as places of refreshment for pilgrims, and provided drink, food and accommodation. Houses of noblemen were also used when the lord was not in residence, which is why so many English inns bear as their

TOP: *Medieval ale house recognizable
by the garland hanging on the pole
above the door.*
BOTTOM: *A medieval tapster.*

25

signpost the arms of the local nobility. Ale houses were
drinking places only, recognized by the sign of the bush
which they hung out on a stick after brewing their ale.
Officials called conners then came to test the ale and passed
it as fit for consumption. This office continued for many
centuries. In Elizabethan times the conners wore leather
pants and tested the strength of the brew by pouring a
sample on a wooden stool and sitting on it. If when they got
up the stool stuck to their breeches, the ale was considered
up to par; if not, the brew was condemned as too weak, and
the tavernkeeper fined for selling inferior ale.

Taverns were frequented by both men and women.
The latter came to drink and gossip, and it was a standard
joke in many of the morality plays of the time that Noah,
having looked everywhere for his wife to get her into the
ark before the deluge, finally finds her in the tavern with
her gossips.

THE BRITISH LIBRARY

People also gathered to drink when some important business was to be transacted, or some social reform celebrated. These get-togethers often took place in the church and were called "ales." There were church ales to collect money for the support of the church, help ales to collect money for the poor, bride ales to help the newlyweds set up house, Easter ales and Whitsun ales. These ales often degenerated into drunken debauches and many a bishop issued decrees against them, but it was not until the Commonwealth that they were finally suppressed.

Not only in Europe was alcohol appreciated. From the thirteenth-century records of Marco Polo, one of the earliest travelers to the East, comes this account:

> Most of the people of Cathay drink wine of the kind that I shall now describe. . . . It is a liquor which they brew of rice, with a quantity of excellent spice in such a fashion that it makes a better drink than any other kind of wine; it is not only good but clear and pleasing to the eye, and being very hot stuff it makes one drunk sooner than any other wine.

The great explorers of the New World found the Mexicans brewing pulque from the maguey century plant, as Diaz reported in 1518, and the conquistadors of Central America and Peru found the natives fermenting *chicha*, a type of beer. As the world opened up in the next three centuries a type of beer was discovered among the people living in the Amazon valley, fermented from the cassava root; in Africa Livingstone came across toddy fermented by the natives from palm sap, while Captain Cook found the Polynesians fermenting *kava* from a kind of pepper. Most of the reports of the drinking customs among these peoples tell of communal drinking and ritual intoxication.

LONICER'S HERBARUM

DISTILLATION

The primitive societies and most of the peoples of antiquity, including the Greeks and the Romans, had only drunk fermented alcohol in the form of wine and beer, that is at a comparatively low alcoholic strength. Now in Europe, in the twelfth century, a new chapter in the history of drink was about to open when the art of distillation was rediscovered. For with the use of the still, an alcoholic beverage three times as strong as wine and beer could be produced. By the thirteenth century, three long treatises had been written on spirits, as the product of the still came to be called, demonstrating that by that time the art of distillation was well understood.

The still was probably invented in the first or second century BC at the school of alchemists in Alexandria, where that famous woman alchemist Mary the Jewess taught.

From the earliest times distillation was
a profession practiced by women, Here
an aquavit woman is distilling some
flavored concoction as can be surmised
by the herbs strewn at her feet.

THE BRITISH LIBRARY

There is no evidence, however, that alcohol was distilled at
this time. Rather the still was used for refining powders.

The word *alcohol* comes from the Arabs, who were
the inheritors of Alexandrian science. *Al-koh'l* was their
word for highly refined powder obtained by distillation, jet
black in color; Arab women used it as a cosmetic to paint
their eyes. (Today in Spain cattle with black rings about
their eyes are called *alcoholado*.) We only adopted the word
alcohol at a much later date to describe what a still
produces.

In the thirteenth century, when the alchemists in
pursuit of their chemical elixirs began to distill fermented
must, the product of the still was called *aqua vitae*, the
water of life: "We call it *aqua vitae* and this name is
remarkably suitable, since it is really a water of immortality. It prolongs life, clears away ill-humor, revives the
heart and maintains youth. . . ." This from Arnauld de
Villeneuve, thirteenth-century professor of medicine at
the University of Montpellier.

By the middle of the thirteenth century the distillation
of spirits from wine was common among the apothecaries
of Italy, who sweetened and spiced the product of the still
to make it enjoyable, thus producing the earliest liqueurs,
and from there the practice spread to France. By the
fifteenth century spirits were distilled from corn in

Germany, where its virtue was questioned: instead of *aqua vitae*, it was known as *schnapsteufel*, the drink of the devil.

By the next century spirits were being distilled on a commercial basis and, especially in Northern Europe, began to replace beer as the common beverage until governments latched onto them as a wonderful source of revenue and taxed them out of reach of the poorer classes.

Brandy was the first spirit to be exported on a large commercial scale: the French distilled large quantities of wine and shipped it off to the Netherlands, the Scandinavian countries and England. Soon all of Northern Europe got into the commercial act. The Dutch were the greatest exporters: their gin found great favor among the English soldiers fighting in the Netherlands. They brought it back to their own country, where soon it was to gives its name to a period that has become infamous in social history: the Gin Era.

By this time the art of distilling had long been practiced in Scotland and Ireland in the late twelfth century. Certainly by the fifteenth century a Scottish monk was known to be distilling *uisge beatha* from malt.

This pungent drink of the Highlands—which came to be known as whisky—was too much for the weaker Sassenach stomach, and in London they continued to drink gin if they were poor, brandy if they were rich (and not at war with France). But in the 1830s a man named Aeneas Coffey perfected a new type of still—the Coffey, patent or continuous still, as it is variously known—which produced a much blander spirit from the traditional malt whisky, and a much cheaper one. This whisky was eventually blended with the more flavorsome malts, and in this guise Scotch whisky started on its conquest of the world market.

The art of brewing and distilling was brought to America by the earliest settlers. Cider was the most common beverage in New England. The Dutch were the earliest distillers, and a distillery was established in Manhattan in 1640, to produce brandywine and gin. It was not these, however, that became the national beverage before the Revolution, but a spirit as yet unheard of in the Old World: rum. When the colonists discovered the hardships of farming the New England soil, they turned to fishing and lumbering. Their fish and wood they then exported to the West Indies, and traded it for rum. Soon it was found more expedient to trade for molasses, and produce the rum at home. It became the prime article of

RADIO TIMES HULTON PICTURE LIBRARY

trade in New England and soon Boston had over forty distilleries as did Rhode Island. Like all spirits rum was considered a medicine, a necessity of life, an essential ration for the troops. It was drunk both at home and in the tavern.

In the new colonies the tavern was the center of community life, as well as a place of rest for the traveler. All important news radiated from it, for often it was the only place in which the local newsletter was available. It was the hub and disseminator of political opinions and indeed of their implementation. Paul Revere and his comrades held their meetings at the Green Dragon in Boston, while Montaigne's Tavern in New York was the headquarters of the Sons of Liberty. Thomas Jefferson drew up the first rough draft of the Declaration of Independence in the Indian Queen Tavern in Philadelphia and Francis Scott Key completed the final verses of the national anthem in a tavern in Baltimore.

After the revolution, towards the end of the century, whiskey began to replace rum, partly because it was distilled from home-grown crops and partly because in 1808 slave trading was abolished, causing the Triangle Trade to collapse. Pennsylvania and Virginia were distilling their rye, Kentucky its corn. Because of the difficulty of transporting bulky sacks of grain, the crops were converted into whiskey to be sold in the eastern markets. Eventually the growth of the industry attracted the notice of Congress, which decided that whiskey would provide a much needed source of revenue, and so, in the 1750s they levied a tax which brought howls of protest

from the farmers. There were public protests and eventually rioting in Pennsylvania, but the so-called Whiskey Rebellion was short-lived and the tax on spirits remained as it had in Europe.

TEMPERANCE

Up until the nineteenth century it was a universal belief that alcohol was a necessity for man. It was necessary for his health, and both young and old partook of it; it was necessary for the worker, who in England was supplied with beer. In America rum was the equivalent worker's spirit. Water, especially in the towns, was scarce, so scarce that there was a whole profession of water carriers; but since water was often unsafe, people tended to drink beverages like beer, which were made with boiled water. (Milk was as expensive as beer and few soft drinks were manufactured before the middle of the century.)

Alcohol was considered an essential part of community work and feasts such as barn raisings, harvest celebrations, weddings and funerals. It played a part in all business deals and day-to-day transactions: shopkeepers offered their best clients a drink in their shops; a drink was exchanged between bargainers to show good will; and a young man might mark the successive stages of his apprenticeship by celebrating with a drink.

But shortly before the turn of the nineteenth century the belief that alcohol was good for you started to be attacked by the medical profession, by industrialists and by various community groups. This was the beginning of the

Both old and young partake in a
French café c. 1879.

MARY EVANS PICTURE LIBRARY

vast temperance movement which swept both England and America, and culminated finally with Prohibition.

In 1784 Dr. Benjamin Rush, a prominent American physician, published a treatise on the harmful effects of spiritous liquors on the human mind and body. Soon he was followed in England by Dr. Lettson who in 1798 published a work on the serious detrimental effects of hard drinking. Their advice was first of all heeded by industrialists running factories, where a sober and steady workforce would quite obviously be of the greatest advantage. In England the earliest antispiritous societies originated in two great textile manufacturing areas, Ulster and Glasgow, soon to be followed by Preston, Bradford and Leeds. In America a group of Connecticut businessmen decided to stop serving rum to their employees and give them beer instead. Industrialists on both sides of the Atlantic were quick to perceive that if they encouraged people to spend less on drink, they would have more money in their pockets to buy manufactured goods.

Prompted by the medical profession and industry, sections of the community began to react against drunkenness and spirits in general. In America the temperance movement was closely backed by the evangelical sects, and its idealistic program to ban all alcoholic beverages soon became a matter for religious and political debate. In England the temperance reforms were more realistic, concentrating on providing remedies for social problems connected with drinking, such as housing and leisure.

The principal focus in both countries was on the saloons and the public houses. These had up to now provided not only a place to drink, but also a center for

Inside the bar at the Edinburgh Castle, one of the earliest coffee palaces. Note the inscription around the bar and the sign at the back of the room which describes it as a "working men's club."

most leisure occupations from dramatics to ratting (the noble sport of pitting your dog against rats). They were a social gathering place, bright, warm and comfortable, in definite contrast to the dreary and dingy homes of many of the people who frequented them. The public house also provided rooms for hire for many friendly, or mutual, societies and other social clubs which were developing at the time.

By the middle of the century the temperance reformers in England had started to establish coffeehouses for working men, and to promote soirées at which soft drinks such as tea and coffee were served. They also agitated for more drinking fountains to be set up in public places. They attacked the licensing laws and in 1854 they managed to get restricted opening hours for pubs. In 1871 they introduced a bill in Parliament which, had it been passed, would have closed down over half the pubs in the country. And in 1886 an act was passed forbidding the sale of beer to children under the age of thirteen.

Together with their negative attitude to alcohol, the temperance movement in England fostered attitudes to replace its attraction: an attempt was made to provide the working classes with more comfortable and alluring homes, and big housing estates rose up all over the country at the end of the century; a move was also made to secure more leisure time by enforcing earlier closing hours in shops, making Saturday a half working day and demanding a bank holiday in August. Lastly, they attempted to provide alternative attractions to the pub in the form of public concerts, libraries, parks and recreation grounds.

The main organ of the temperance movement was the British and Foreign Temperance Society, which was very much influenced by American temperance ideas borne over on the wave of international philanthropy at the beginning of the century.

The social achievement of the temperance movement in England was far reaching, but its actual success in curtailing the consumption of alcohol was minimal. During the first forty years of the movement, per capita consumption actually increased, and there was no appreciable decline in the ratio of drinking places to population.

The reverse was true in the US: the temperance movement was less overtly concerned with social improvements, but it did manage to achieve national prohibition. As in England, medical opinion and the support of the industrial bosses did much to prepare the way for the temperance movement, but its main impulse came from the evangelical doctrine that drink is the devil's own gift.

The first temperance society in the United States was organized by the pastor of the First Congregational Church of Moreau, in Saratoga County. In 1808 its forty-odd members pledged to: "use no rum, gin, whisky, wine or any distilled spirits . . . except by the advice of a physician, or in case of actual disease, also excepting wine at public dinners." This was soon followed by the Connecticut Society for the Reformation of Morals, led by the Reverend Lyman Beecher, who was intent on suppressing gambling as well as alcohol. His sermons were distributed throughout the country and had an enormous impact. In 1826 he founded the American Society for the Promotion of Temperance, later called the American Temperance Union. Led by Protestant clergymen, its members were at first required to take the pledge to abstain from spirits, but by 1836 it required "total abstinence from all that can intoxicate." The union was not only interested in promoting abstinence among its supporters, but also in promoting a legislature to forbid the production and sale of alcohol in every state.

One outstanding exception to religiously inspired temperance movements was the Washington Temperance Society founded in 1840, which made no reference to God or the Devil in their lectures, but told most vividly of the horrors of drunkenness from personal experience, for it was a society of reformed drunkards. Their success was startling—within the first few months they had enrolled over a thousand members—but, unfortunately, it was

TOP: *"Bringing back the rum." A US temperance cartoon.*

BOTTOM: *Temperance broadside, c. 1840s, lampooning a New England rum distillery.*

short-lived. As the Washingtonians had no interest in promoting a prohibitionist legislature, they therefore never gained the support of other temperance movements nor, more important still, that of the politicians.

In the meantime, the temperance societies that were politically active moved steadily and surely towards their goal throughout the rest of the century. By 1833 they had persuaded the Supreme Court to rule that state governments could regulate their own liquor trade; in 1851 Maine passed the first statewide prohibition law, soon followed by thirteen more states; in 1869 a Prohibition party was organized, running its own candidates for election. In 1874 the Women's Christian Temperance Union was founded, followed in 1893 (again at a First Congregational Church in Oberlin, Ohio) by the most potent and politically active temperance union, the Anti-Saloon League, which was to sweep the nation to Prohibition.

Temperance propaganda was abundant and varied, and included songs, sermons, plays and demonstration marches. Women took a very active part in campaigning for the abolition of the saloon, and one woman in particular, Carry Nation, actually achieved notoriety by going about demolishing saloons with her now-famous hatchet.

Children, too, were enlisted in the fight. Their elders taught them slogans and songs and sent them to march and sing around the polling booths:

Think of sisters, wives and mothers
of helpless babes in some low slum,
Think not of yourselves, but others,
Vote against the Demon Rum.

They were also indoctrinated at school. The Women's Christian Temperance Union instituted a Department of Scientific Temperance Instruction, and by 1902 every state except Arizona had a law requiring temperance to be taught in public schools. Temperance text books were published which preached that all alcohol is dangerous and a seductive poison, that fermentation turns beer and wine and cider from food into poison, and that by its very nature a little alcohol will create an appetite for more and lead to crime and final degradation.

But the deciding factor that won the day for the prohibitionists was the war hysteria of 1917. Liquor was

TOP: *The 1870s: Fashionable ladies in London enjoying a tipple while trying on hats at their favorite milliner's.*
BOTTOM: *Fashionable American ladies of the same period praying outside a saloon to banish the demon rum.*

PLEDGE of the
Woman's Christian Temperance Union

☞ PLEDGE ☜

I hereby solemnly promise, GOD HELPING ME, to abstain from all distilled, fermented and malt liquors, including wine, beer and cider; and to employ all proper means to discourage the use of, and traffic in the same.

After signing this Pledge, retain it, but send name to Mrs. Geo. F. Pashley, 629 McDonough St., Brooklyn, N. Y., State Supt. work among Soldiers and Sailors.

Name .....

Date ....

"GOOD HEAVENS! ARE YOU THE DEMON RUM?"
"NO; I'M THE ANGEL PROHIBITION."

seen as an evil, for it prevented American soldiers from doing their duty; beer was unpatriotic, as it was mostly brewed by Germans; brewing used up 11 million loaves of barley a day which could be better used for feeding the starving Allies. In simplistic terms the dry folk were for God and America and against the saloon and Germany, while the wets supported the Devil and the Germans against their country. A resolution to introduce a prohibition amendment to the Constitution was put to the Sixty-fifth Congress which convened in March 1917, and not long after the Eighteenth Amendment was passed by a vote of 282 to 128. Thirty-six states ratified the amendment in a little less than a year, and on January 16, 1919, it was officially adopted. In October of that year, Representative Andrew J. Volstead of Minnesota introduced the National Prohibition Act, better known as the Volstead Act, to enforce the Eighteenth Amendment.

In the meantime everyone who could afford it bought up drink and laid by stores . . . and Prohibition Eve parties were held at all the smart hotels.

The age of Prohibition had begun, and the great Virginian evangelist, Bill Sunday, began to preach:

> The slums will soon be only a memory. We will turn our prisons into factories and our jails into storehouses and corncribs. Men will walk upright now, women will smile, and the children will laugh.

The government set up a Prohibition Bureau and appointed a Prohibition Commissioner to enforce the Volstead Act. He proclaimed that: "We shall see that [liquor] is not manufactured, nor sold nor given away, nor hauled in anything on the surface of the earth or under the earth or in the air." Did he intentionally not mention water? Yachts, fishing trawlers, and any other kind of boat were at once converted into rumrunners to smuggle in supplies of liquor supposedly on its way to the West Indies from Europe. These vessels rode at anchor along Rum Row, along the Atlantic and Gulf coasts just outside US territorial waters. They supplied the smaller speedcraft with liquor to be smuggled ashore.

Rumrunning soon became a profession, and one of the most professional of the lot was Captain Bill McCoy, who boasted that he only imported unadulterated spirits—the "real McCoy."

TOP: *Ben Shahn's Prohibition mural.*
BOTTOM: *Picketing of a rum-laden schooner off Rum Row.*
OFFICIAL U.S. COAST GUARD PATROL.

41

What could not be imported was manufactured from practically anything: industrial alcohol (which was still legal); wood alcohol; and the notorious Jamaican ginger, which was distilled into a type of whiskey which could eventually cause paralysis of the legs and feet—over 15,000 Americans were crippled by it during Prohibition. Moonshine poured out of illegal stills and bathtub gin was manufactured in increasing amounts. New York alone had over 13,000 speak-easies—illegal drinking places where customers had to whisper a password before they would be admitted. With bootlegging, crime also flourished and soon huge gangs of gangsters led by such legendary figures as Al Capone and Legs Diamond had virtual control of the liquor trade and the speak-easies.

LICENSED BEVERAGE INDUSTRIES LTD.

As it became increasingly apparent that Prohibition was impossible to enforce, more and more associations were formed to have the Eighteenth Amendment repealed. In his 1932 presidential campaign Franklin D. Roosevelt promised that it would be revoked. Having won the election, he at once had the Volstead Act amended to allow the sale of beer, and a year after his election the Twenty-first Amendment was ratified, repealing Prohibition. People everywhere rejoiced as what Herbert Hoover had called an "experiment noble in purpose" finally came to an end.

MODERN ATTITUDES AND TRENDS

Today in a few countries, notably the Muslim and Hindu nations, alcohol is not (supposedly) consumed. But in most countries throughout the world it is still retained as the traditional symbol of hospitality. We drink at every conceivable occasion, from family gatherings to state banquets.

And we also drink to relax. Alcohol is still, after all, society's most acceptable drug. For most people an evening drink marks the switching point between a day of work and an evening of leisure. The cocktail hour is a long-established custom in America, and it has gradually spread throughout the world, accounting in part for the rise in consumption of spirits in traditionally wine-drinking countries.

But there is also a new trend in the wind, or rather a revival of another century's ways: connoisseurship, the appreciation of taste in alcohol. More and more people are beginning to have a drink not because it relaxes them or makes them feel good, but because they like the taste of it. I quote from a statement by Jack Yogman, president of Seagram's, to Lammy Johnstone in a recent article published in *Mainliner*: "You know, the American people are finally waking up to taste. If my theory is correct, we will be more successful in the years ahead selling our customers with brands that have taste, not bland liquors."

At the turn of the last century customers had started to demand, or producers had started to promote—it's difficult to say which was chicken here and which was egg—a blander spirit than had previously been marketed. The most obvious example of this made its appearance in the Scotch whisky trade in 1923, when Berry Bros. & Rudd launched their famous Cutty Sark brand and heavily promoted it as a "light" whisky. (The term light refers primarily to taste and not to color, although the two go hand in hand, as we shall see.)

The light whisky trend developed into a fashion for the blander, less distinctly flavored spirits than the old-fashioned heavy brandies, whiskies and rums. (Blandness or "lightness," by the way, should not be confused with alcoholic strength: the blandest of all alcohol is neutral spirit—190 US proof.) The 1950s saw the meteoric boom of the lightest of all spirits, vodka. This was followed by the ever-steady rise of the sales of light Bacardi rum, now the largest-selling brand of any spirit in the world; and in 1972 America marketed a new type of whiskey, called tellingly "light whiskey."

Hand in hand with the demand for light-tasting spirits went the demand for light-*looking* ones.

Now color in spirits is an acquired characteristic. Today most commercial spirits that are colored have a minute amount of caramel added to them prior to bottling. At the moment of distillation all spirits, whether they be brandy, whisk(e)y, rum or vodka, are colorless. Heavy, flavorful spirits, such as brandy, bourbon, and Scotch require maturing in a wooden barrel to let the flavor of the spirit develop (see "Alcohol: How is it made?" for a more detailed explanation). As a particular spirit matures, it acquires a certain hue from the wood. Thus: the deeper the hue, the older the spirit, *and* the more mellow the taste. Consequently, in the days before light spirits came into vogue, color used to be an indication of age, taste, and therefore quality.

But with the trend toward light spirits, for a growing

number of commercial spirits, maturing for long periods, if at all, was no longer as necessary as it was in the past, and color began to lose its premium. In fact, it was frowned upon, because it suggested a strongly flavored spirit. People began looking for straw-colored whisky, colorless gin and vodka, and white (not dark) rum.

Of course, light spirits do have their place. They are wonderful as mixers, for example, and Bacardi has thrived on advertising itself as "the mixable one." They are delightful in combination with fruit juices, soft drinks or in a sparkling party punch.

But it is good to see that taste is coming back into its own, for, on the right occasion, what can give more exquisite pleasure than sipping a really fine, well-aged cognac or a rich Scotch malt whisky?

CODA

It is illegal to distill without a license in many countries. Wine and beer you may brew at home with the blessing of the law upon your head, but distill spirits you may not, and a dreadful thing it is to be found in the possession of a worm, that distinctive coil-shaped pipe so vital to the home still. To whit the following:

A man was hauled up before a judge charged with distilling without a license.

"What proof of this charge?" boomed His Lordship.

"This, m'lud," replied the prosecuting counsel, "was found on his premises." And he indicated Exhibit A, unmistakably a worm.

"Case proved," said the judge. "Does the defendant have anything further to add?"

"Yes, m'lud. I would also like to plead guilty to rape."

"You would like to do what?" exclaimed the astonished judge.

"If you please, m'lud. Though I have the instrument to do both, I have done neither."

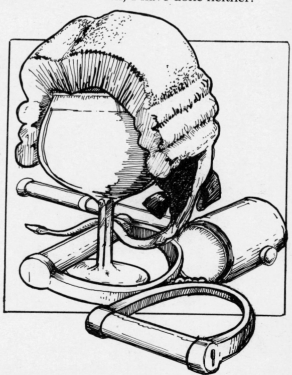

Alcohol:
How is it made?

ALCOHOL is made by microscopic plants called yeasts. These tiny organisms which exist almost everywhere in thousands of varieties quite spontaneously attack the sugar in any solution (the juice of fruits, the sap of plants, milk, wild honey, etc.) and provided that the temperature is moderate, they change the sugar into a colorless liquid called alcohol: ethyl alcohol, the kind we drink. This natural process is known as fermentation.

Two groups of raw materials may be acted upon by the yeasts to produce alcohol by fermentation: *sugary substances*, such as fruit, sugar cane, agave, honey, milk; and *starchy substances*, such as wheat, corn (maize), rye, rice, potatoes. The crops harvested in a given area will often determine what is drunk in that area. In grape-growing countries one will drink wine and brandy; in corn-growing countries, beer and whisky; in sugar-cane areas, rum. In some regions major crops of fruit, rice, cactus and palm trees abound, and from them fruit brandies, rice spirits, tequila and arak are produced.

To ferment sugary substances, it is merely necessary to crush them in order to extract the juice and then let the yeasts go to work. To make wine, for instance, the grapes are harvested in autumn when they are ripe, and carried to the wine press. On each grape there will be some ten million wild yeasts ready to turn the grape juice into wine; about 100,000 wine yeasts ready to carry on the job where the wild yeasts leave off; and about 100,000 bacteria ready to turn the wine into vinegar.

Once upon a time the grapes were piled in shallow wooden troughs and trodden with bare feet to break the skins and extract the juice of the fruit. (Care had to be taken not to crush the pips, which would give the wine a bitter taste.) The must, as the unfermented juice is called, along with the pulp and skins was then poured into the large vats where the wild yeasts, coming into contact with the sugar in the pulp of the grape, would start the fermentation process. During fermentation, as the yeasts convert the sugar into alcohol, carbon dioxide is produced, and this gas, escaping from the liquid, causes the fierce bubbling and boiling characteristic of a fermenting brew. Fermentation proceeds until a solution of about 4 percent alcohol is reached, at which point the wild yeasts die off. The wine yeasts then take over and carry on the fermentation until the alcohol content reaches 16–18 percent, when they too are killed, or else have used up all the sugar supply. After this the bacteria take over and start converting the wine into vinegar.

Nowadays a machine both destalks and crushes the grapes, replacing the bare feet, while the wild yeasts and bacteria are eliminated by sulphuring. Sulphur dioxide is added to the must to produce a coating on top of the vat which seals the must from contact with the air. Wild yeasts and bacteria need air in order to operate, while wine yeasts are quite happy carrying on their job in the airless must, provided that the temperature is between 5°–30° C (41°–86° F) and the alcohol content below 18 percent, after which the yeasts will die, leaving behind the must which has been converted into wine.

Starchy crops on the other hand need some preliminary preparation before fermentation can begin. The starch has to be converted into sugar. The most common way of doing this is by malting, which is a process of artificial germination. Take beer, for example. Beer is made from barley. In order to convert the starch in the barley to sugar, the barley is soaked for up to sixty hours in water and is then spread on the floor of the malting house to germinate. In Ireland, in the production of whiskey, this is charmingly called "fooling the barley," because the process of germination is foiled almost as soon as it has begun by heating and drying the sprouting seed. But during the short time the seed is allowed to grow, it develops enzymes, organic substances which act as catalysts; the most important is diastase, which converts the moist starch into soluble sugar. These enzymes are produced in quantities far beyond that which is necessary to convert the starch in the individual grain so that even a small quantity of malted barley can convert large amounts of starchy material, approximately ten times its own weight, into sugar. Once the starch has been converted into sugar, yeast is added to start fermentation which makes the vats bubble and froth as the sugar is changed into alcohol and carbon dioxide, which escapes from the seething mass.

Fermented wines and beer contain only between 3 and 18 percent alcohol by volume. How then is the stronger stuff made? The answer is by distillation.

All fermented alcoholic brews are solutions of alcohol in water. Distilling is the process of separating the alcohol from the water. This can be done by heating because the boiling point of alcohol is lower than that of water. Thus if wine or beer is heated to a temperature somewhere between 78.5° C (141.3° F) and 100° C (212° F)—the

DISTILLERS COMPANY LTD.

respective boiling points of alcohol and water—the alcohol
will vaporize and separate off from the water. It can then be
recondensed into a liquid, which is of much higher
alcoholic strength than the original fermented brew from
which it is distilled. The distillate is called a spirit.

In the sixteenth century a spirit was said to be
proven—i.e., that it contained a palatable amount of
alcohol in the solution (proof spirit)—if it ignited in a
certain way when mixed with gunpowder. If the mixture
flared up, it was thought to be too strong; and if it remained
a sizzling soggy mess, it was too weak; but if it burned with
a steady flame—*voilà!* a proven spirit. Hence our term
proof, which has come to indicate the amount of alcohol in a
beverage.

Nowadays the methods of testing the strength of a
beverage are more precise, but the issue has become highly
complicated by the fact that different countries have
adopted different systems. The metric system, used widely
throughout Europe, is called Gay-Lussac and is the
simplest. 100° represents absolute alcohol and all other
strengths are expressed as percentages, so that 50° Gay-

Lussac means that the spirit contains 50 percent alcohol. In the US absolute alcohol is 200° and 100° is proof spirit so that if you halve the given proof, say 80°, it contains 40 percent alcohol. In the British or Sikes system 175° (a rounded figure) is absolute alcohol, 100° proof spirit, which is 57.1 percent alcohol by volume, an awkward figure to deal with. Mercifully by 1977 Great Britain will have abandoned its complicated Sikes system of computations in favor of the simpler method of calculating strength by percentage of alcohol per volume. A simplified comparison table is on p. 158.

Proof is not only important on the label of your bottle to tell you how strong your drink is. It is all-important at the time of distillation. If you were to take a mash of fruit, a mash of grain and one of molasses, and distill all three to a very high proof, say 190° US, the three distillates would all taste very much the same—that is, they would have practically no taste or aroma and it would be hard to tell which was which. If on the other hand all three mashes were distilled at a lower proof, say below 160° US, you would have three distinct spirits: brandy, whisky and rum. This is because the lower the proof to which a liquor is distilled, the greater will be the proportion of congeners which come over in—and contribute to the distinctive flavor of—the distillate. This is why US law stipulates that bourbon, to be bourbon, must be distilled at or below 160° US in order to retain the congeners that are characteristic of the spirit. Were it to be distilled at a higher proof, say 190° US, all congeners would be eliminated and the distillate would be a neutral spirit.

Congeners are what makes whisky different from rum and rum different from brandy. The term is the collective name for other alcohols and small characteristic compounds that together with ethyl alcohol are found in all alcoholic beverages and which develop during distillation and aging in wood. They include: fusel oils, which are the higher alcohols such as propyl, butyl, amyl and others; esters, which are produced by the combination of alcohols with acids and provide the distinctive aroma of the liquor; and aldehydes. When present in excessive quantities, congeners are considered impurities and will impart a disagreeable smell and flavor to the distillate. If totally eliminated the distillate will lose all character. Therefore to maintain them at a desirable level is the major challenge to the distiller's skill.

A spirit rich in congeners such as malt whisky or

cognac require a specially long aging period in wood to allow the congeners to develop, while a spirit like vodka, distilled at a very high proof so that almost every trace of congeners has been removed, requires no aging at all. There are, for instance, only 33 milligrams of congeners in a liter of vodka, which is not aged, and anything from 500 milligrams to 2,600 milligrams of congeners in whisky or cognac.

So, distilling to a low proof (say, under 160° US) produces a spirit high in congeners and rich in body and taste, while distilling to a high proof produces a spirit low in congeners and light in body and taste, while distilling at a very high proof (say, 190° US or above) produces a neutral spirit with virtually no aroma or taste.

The degree of proof to which a spirit is distilled is in some cases, like that of malt whisky and cognac, determined by the apparatus employed. There are basically two types of apparatus used in distilling: the pot still, an adaptation of the original stills used in the sixteenth century; and the patent or continuous still, adapted from the Coffey still, an invention of the early 1830s.

DISTILLATION BY POT STILL

The pot still is a large, bulbous copper pot narrowing at the top into a long thin neck which is connected to a coiled pipe called the worm. This lies inside a jacket of cold water which condenses the alcohol vapor.

Pot-still distillation is accomplished in two or three stages with the distillate at each stage undergoing a further redistillation to remove more and more of the congeneric impurities and produce a purer spirit. After each batch is finished the pot must be emptied and cleaned before the next batch is distilled.

The first batch of fermented brew, known as the wash, is heated in the pot until all the alcohol in the pot has vaporized and passed up through the neck into the worm. The condensed vapor is then collected in a receiving vessel. About one-third of the original volume of wash is collected. This "low wines," as it is called in Scotland—or *brouillis* in the Cognac region—is now ready to be distilled in a second still, which is usually smaller than the first. The first vapors to come off contain too high a proportion of impurities and are thus discarded into a special receiver. These are the poisonous "heads" or "foreshots," as they are called in Scotland. When the purer alcohol starts coming over, the stillman switches the stream of liquid into

another receiver. This is the middle run, the good "heart" of the spirit, known in the rum trade as the *madilla*. Towards the end of the distillation the fusel oils will start to come over too strong. So the stillman again switches the spirit back into the first receiver. These final discarded vapors are known to the Scotch whisky trade as the "tails" or "feints."

Besides being used to distill spirits high in congeners like cognac and malt whisky, a type of pot still is also used for flavoring spirits such as gin. The neutral spirit is redistilled through a tray containing herbs, plants, seeds, etc., and carries over into the distillate the flavor it has picked up from the tray.

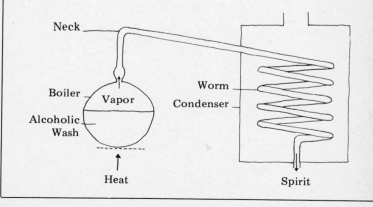

BACARDI LTD.

DISTILLATION BY PATENT OR CONTINUOUS STILL

The other type of still, the patent or continuous still, is a tall cylinder which rises through two or three stories of the distillery. There are many variations of this type of still—the diagram gives the basic idea of how it works.

The continuous still is composed of the two interconnecting copper columns called the analyzer and the rectifier, both of which are subdivided horizontally by perforated copper plates or trays. The cold wash (fermented liquor drawn off from the mash of grain) is introduced into the top of the rectifier (A). As it journeys down in a tube in the column it is heated by the hot vapors (F) entering the base of the rectifier (B). Good and hot it is piped into the analyzer (C)—also known as the stripper column—where it travels downward from tray to tray. As it does so, the steam which has been injected under pressure at the base

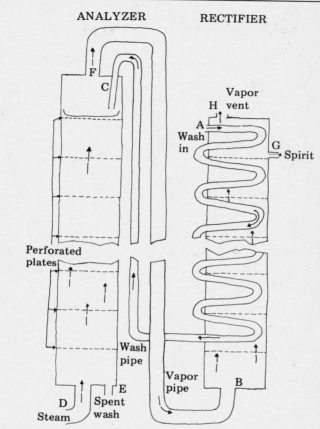

ANALYZER RECTIFIER

F
C

Vapor
H vent
A
Wash
in
G
Spirit

Perforated
plates

Wash
pipe

Vapor
pipe B

D E
Steam Spent
wash

of this column (D) rises through the wash and strips it of its
alcohol by converting the latter into vapor and thus
separating it from the water in the wash. The spent wash is
drawn off at the bottom (E). The alcohol vapor now passes
back into the rectifier (F to B) and as it rises up it is
cooled by the cold wash descending through the column in
its tube, which causes the vapor to condense on the
horizontal plates. On the lower plates, any water still
present in the vapor condenses and is drawn off.
Continuing up the column, and getting cooler as it goes,
the vapor will reach a level where its temperature will be
about 185°F. Here the fusel oils separate out, condense and
are dried off. Further up, the vapor reaches a point where
the temperature is about 178° and here (G) the ethyl
alcohol will condense and be drawn off into the spirit safe
while the remaining vapor of alcohol containing a high
concentration of aldehydes will continue to rise and be
drawn off at the top of the column (H) to be reprocessed.

The patent still has three commercial advantages over

the pot still. The still does not have to be emptied after a "batch" and can therefore produce more rapidly greater quantities of alcohol. Secondly, it affords a great saving in fuel because the vapors heat the fermented liquor to make it vaporize. And, above all, this type of still can in one session, so to speak, produce a far purer spirit than the pot still for it provides a continuous process of distillation: the spirit is distilled and distilled and further distilled. As the alcohol vapor rises up the rectifier, it condenses into liquid and falls back to the bottom of the column. Here it is once again heated and revaporized, to rise once more and start the process all over again.

AGING

The last step in the production of spirits is aging. The time required for aging will depend on the congener content of the spirit. A spirit rich in congeners will require a long maturing period in wood, during which time the oxygen in the air seeps through the pores of the wood to affect the spirit, increasing its aroma and mellowing the taste, while the spirit absorbs some of the tannin in the wood and acquires a golden tinge. Some cognacs are aged up to fifty years, some malt whiskies up to twenty-five, heavy Jamaican rums up to fifteen, and the lighter ones up to four. Gin and vodka are not aged. Unlike wine, once the spirit has been bottled in glass it no longer ages. As far as color is concerned, a tiny amount can be picked up from the wood, but the golden spirits are generally colored by the addition of small amounts of caramel.

A blender works primarily by his sense of smell. He "noses" his sample in a tulip-shaped glass and judges whether each element of the spirit is fully matured and ready for blending. He will be able to "nose" a row of bottles like this in about ten minutes.

THE DISTILLERS COMPANY LTD.

The final step in the production of many distilled spirits, such as brandy, whisk(e)y and rum, is blending. The most important factor of a blend is that it should be consistent in flavor and quality.

Like distilling, blending is an art. It does not consist in mixing a large amount of inferior produce with a small amount of superior quality in the hopes that the amalgam will improve. The purpose of blending is to draw out the best quality of each component spirit, every one of which is chosen to enhance the other.

The blender takes a sample from each component of his formula, "noses" it for quality and determines the proportions of each ingredient for the required formula. After the blender has approved the samples the appropriate casks are poured into huge troughs which flow into the blending vats where the blend is "roused" by compressed air and thoroughly mixed. It is then poured back into casks and matured for a further period.

From
to the Harvey

Liqueurs:
Apothecaries
Wallbanger

FERMENTED liquor is the work of nature. Man has certainly improved upon it with his knowledge of chemistry, but basically it is a phenomenon which occurs without his help. Distilled spirits, on the other hand, are the result of man's ingenuity.

Spirits originated in the workshop of the alchemist, that half-doctor/half-witch of the Middle Ages, who was searching for that which all men have wondered about: the secret of immortality. The first men to distill a spirit thought that they had found the magic elixir, and they called it *aqua vitae*, the water of life. It didn't come up to expectations, but it did the next best thing: promoted health and long life—or so they believed for many centuries. Indeed, it was not until the twentieth century that spirits were banished from pride of place in the medicine cabinet.

And so the history of spirits moved from the alchemist's laboratory to the shops of the apothecaries, who used it as the basic solution for their medicinal herbs, to make tonics, digestives and analgesics for the treatment of all pains big and small, from the Black Death to childbirth.

Like all medicine before the invention of pills, spirits sold better if they were palatable. So they were sweetened and spiced (the main characteristics of a liqueur as we shall see), and so agreeable did the spirits become that people started drinking them for pleasure. "Freelier than is profitable to their health they take and drink [them]," a Dutch physician acidly commented regarding his fellow countrymen in 1550.

Besides the apothecaries, the great herbalists of the Middle Ages were the monks, who were literate, had ready access to ancient treatises on medicine, and also had the leisure to experiment. Today throughout Europe many monasteries still produce their own particular elixir according to age-old recipes. But only one monastic order produces a liqueur on a large commercial scale—the Carthusian monks of the Grande Chartreuse, who distill their green Chartreuse liqueur from a seventeenth-century recipe.

The art of distilling spirits and compounding liqueurs probably started in Italy, possibly at Salerno, the great early university of medical science. From Italy the art of compounding liqueurs passed to France and one of the most famous liqueurs—the *rossolis*, from roses, aniseed, fennel, dill and coriander—was a favorite *digestif* of Louis XIV.

A sixteenth-century visualization of the
alchemist at work.

THE MANSELL COLLECTION

During the Renaissance many "waters" were distilled, and the still room was an integral part of every
household, the domain of the lady of the house. Distilled
spirits were used both for cosmetics and for medical
purposes, as well as for pleasure. Rosewater was a well-
known tonic for the complexion; water of cloves, a
distillation to alleviate stomach ache, obesity and worms.

From Italy in 1749 a young man came to London. His
name was Giacomo Justerini, and he brought with him a
secret and most complex recipe for an Aqua Mirablis and
various other formulas for making liqueurs. Soon he was
doing a flourishing trade as a wine merchant from the shop
"two doors below the Opera House in the Haymarket," as
was advertised in the *Morning Post* of June 17, 1779. The
shop still stands with the firm's well-known name of

*The largest liqueur cellar in the world:
the Carthusian monks at work in the
Hall of herbs and cellar of the
Chartreuse distiller.*

Justerini & Brooks above the door, a firm which in the next century was to launch the famous J&B blend of Scotch whisky.

The word *liqueur* (also known as a "cordial" in the United States) comes from the Latin *liquefacere* (to dissolve), and indeed liqueurs are not so much characterized by the alcohol on which they are based—usually a neutral alcohol, a brandy, or in some cases a whisky—as by what is "dissolved" in that alcohol. Flavoring substances are usually "dissolved" in alcohol in one of three ways in the production of liqueurs: by maceration, distillation or percolation. Maceration consists of soaking the flavoring substances—herbs, fruits, seeds, leaves—in alcohol so that the liquid becomes impregnated with the flavor and aroma of the plant; the product that results is called an infusion. For distillation the flavoring substances are placed in a basket suspended in a pot still, and the alcohol is distilled through them, so that the vapors carry the flavor and aroma of the distillate. Percolation is a method commonly used when the flavoring substances are beans (cocoa, coffee) or pods (vanilla). The alcohol slowly drips through the beans to capture their flavor in the same way as one makes coffee.

Liqueurs are also characterized by their sweetness. In France the minimum sugar content is two hundred grams of sugar per liter, while the liqueurs which are called *crèmes* must contain at least four hundred grams of sugar per liter.

After a distillate has been sweetened it is diluted to bring it down to market strength, usually between 25 and 45 percent. It then may be colored—indeed much of the appeal of liqueurs is surely due to their brilliance. Infusion of plants are usually used for this purpose: blackcurrants for a violet hue, saffron for a yellow, mint for a green, cherries for a red and various blends for in-between shades.

The flavoring substances of liqueurs can be grouped under the following headings: herbs and spices; seeds and plants; and fruits.

HERBS AND SPICES

Unlike fruit liqueurs which rely mostly on a single fruit for their flavor, herbal liqueurs are a complex blend of such flavors as cumin, ginger, mint, nutmeg, thyme and vanilla, together with the less well-known flavors of angelica, gentian root, hyssop, wild flowers and many others. The number of ingredients vary from a few to over a hundred and their proportion, method of preparation and final

blending are kept secret by each producer, so that only a general account can be given of the following major herb and spice liqueurs.

BÉNÉDICTINE is produced at Fécamp in Normandy and is flavored with over twenty herbs, including angelica, balm, cinnamon, cloves, juniper berries, nutmeg, tea and vanilla, some of which are distilled, others macerated in neutral alcohol. The flavored distillates are then aged and eventually blended. The liqueur is then colored dark amber by the addition of caramel and a little saffron. The original recipe belonged to the Bénédictine monks, and each bottle of the liqueur bears the initial of their religious maxim: DOM, *Deo Optimo, Maximo* (to God, most good, most high). In 1938, following the trend towards less sweet liqueurs, the firm launched a product called B&B, Bénédictine and brandy, a blend of about 60 percent Bénédictine and 40 percent cognac.

BRONTË is a light amber-colored, medium-sweet, spicy liqueur produced in Yorkshire, the home of the famous Brontë novelists.

CENTERBE is an Italian liqueur based on neutral spirits and flavored with over one hundred herbs, hence its name.

CHARTREUSE is a liqueur produced at Voiron in France by the Carthusian brothers of the Grande Chartreuse. Actually only three brothers are released from their monastic duties to perform this task at the distillery, a short distance from the monastery. Only they are allowed into the Hall of Herbs, where the ingredients are weighed and compounded. The brothers produce two types of Chartreuse, a green and a yellow. The former, which is distilled according to a seventeenth-century recipe, calls for over 130 different ingredients to be treated by five successive infusions and four separate distillations. In 1838 the yellow

Chartreuse was created, somewhat sweeter and less complex than the green.

GALLIANO, originally produced in Livorno, is now made on a much larger scale at Solaro, near Milan from herbs distilled in neutral alcohol, and is colored a pastel shade of yellow. Although sold in Italy, it is far more popular in America as an ingredient of the Harvey Wallbanger.

IZARRA is Basque liqueur, which can either be green or yellow. The green variety contains over forty ingredients, the yellow thirty, among which is the wild elder flower which grows in the Pyrenees. Some of the herbs are distilled in neutral alcohol, and some macerated in alcohol and armagnac. It is aged for six months before being sweetened and colored.

STREGA is Italian for "the witch." The sharp-tasting liqueur is produced in Benevento in southern Italy and has a vivid yellow color.

TRAPPISTINE is an armagnac-based liqueur flavored with herbs.

VIEILLE CURE is a green or yellow liqueur produced near Bordeaux from over fifty ingredients macerated in neutral alcohol which is then aged for up to three years.

SEEDS AND PLANTS

Most seed and plant liqueurs are dominated by one particular flavor—anise, chocolate, coffee, almond, cumin, etc.—but like the herbal liqueurs the best of these are rendered more complex by the supporting flavors of other plants and spices to which they are blended in a harmonious whole.

Some of the following liqueurs are generic, others proprietary brands.

Aniseed

ANIS is the generic name for a brandy or neutral spirit flavored with aniseed, the oil of which turns milky when diluted with water.

ANISETTE is flavored with aniseed. It is the specialty of a very famous French liqueur firm, Marie Brizard (now Marie Brizard et Roger), who founded the business in 1775 with this very liqueur. The company now produces thirty-four other liqueurs, but anisette is still their most important. The aniseed is distilled in neutral alcohol and blended with the distillate of sixteen other seeds and plants. Other firms like Arrow, Cusenier, Garnier and Rocher produce aniseed liqueurs of varying sweetness and subtlety.

Sambuca is an Italian liqueur that tastes of aniseed, though in fact the flavor comes from the *Sambucus nigra*, a type of elder bush. It is traditionally drunk with two or three coffee beans floating on the surface. The liquid is set alight for a few seconds to allow the coffee to impart its flavor.

Caraway and Cumin

Cumin Liquidium Optimum Castelli is a white Danish liqueur flavored with caraway and cumin: "the best caraway liqueur in the castle."

Kümmel is a northern European clear liqueur flavored with caraway and cumin seeds distilled in neutral alcohol. Allasch Kümmel is a very high-quality product of this liqueur; while Eiskümmel is a special variety, bottled while still warm so that sugar crystals form at the base of the bottle. German kümmel is very dry and often drunk as an *aperitif*.

Chocolate

Crème de cacao is made by distilling cocoa beans in neutral alcohol and combining this distillate with an infusion of vanilla pods. It is produced by most French liqueur firms and by many firms in America including Leroux and Hiram Walker.

Cheri-suisse is a liqueur produced by Seagrams. It combines the flavor of chocolate with that of cherries.

Choclair is an American liqueur produced by Arrow combining the flavor of chocolate and coconut.

Marmot Chocolate is a Swiss liqueur flavored with cocoa beans. Its distinctive feature is the pieces of chocolate which float about in it.

Royal Mint-Chocolate Liqueur is marketed by the English firm of Hallgarten; it combines the flavor of rich chocolate with that of fresh mint.

Sabra is a liqueur from Israel flavored with cocoa beans and bitter oranges.

Vandermint is a Dutch liqueur flavored with cocoa beans and mint; it is very sweet and heavy.

Coffee

Crème de mocha is flavored with coffee beans. Although a *crème*, and therefore extra sweet, it tastes less sweet on account of the bitter flavor of the beans.

Kahlua is a Mexican liqueur flavored with coffee beans. It is very sweet with a strong coffee flavor.

Tia Maria is a rum-based Jamaican liqueur flavored with coffee beans, not too sweet or sticky.

Mint

CRÈME DE MENTHE is produced by most liqueur firms, usually from a variety of mints separately distilled and then blended. Other mint liqueurs are marketed under various names such as: FREEZOMINT, MENTA SACCO and PIPPERMINT. Often they are served over shaved ice and sometimes tipped with soda as a long *aperitif*.

Nut

The nut-like flavor in most liqueurs is usually that of almond. Often, however, this almond flavor does not come from the almond nut at all but from the kernel, or inside of the pit, of a fruit such as an apricot, a cherry or a sloe.

AMARETTO DI SARONNO is an Italian liqueur made from neutral alcohol distilled with apricot pits together with various aromatic herbs. The flavor of the liqueur is that of crushed almonds, and the liqueur takes its name from *amaretti*, little biscuits dotted with slivers of almonds.

CRÈME DE NOISETTE is a liqueur flavored with hazelnuts.

CRÈME DE NOYAUX is generally flavored with various fruit pits and almond extract.

PRUNELLE comes in two varieties: one made from the fruit of the sloe and the other from its kernel. The latter has the distinctive nutty almond flavor.

Tea

Tea-flavored liqueurs are much less fashionable than they used to be and today tea is mostly used as a supporting flavor in the production of certain liqueurs.

SUNTORY GREEN TEA LIQUEUR is a Japanese product made from different varieties of tea leaves macerated in a blend of brandy and neutral alcohol and heavily sweetened.

Vanilla

PARFAIT AMOUR is a very sweet liqueur of a striking violet hue with a pervading flavor of vanilla. It is, however, also flavored with citrus peel, roses, almond, coriander and other spices.

Violets

CRÈME YVETTE is a violet-blue liqueur produced in the United States, flavored with Parma violets and named after Yvette Guilbert, the famous cabaret singer of the 1890s.

FRUITS

Fruit liqueurs are made by flavoring neutral alcohol or brandy and adding sugar. They are not to be confused with fruit brandies, proper *eaux de vie*, which are made by fermenting the fruit and distilling the fermentation, as is done in the production of *kirsch* (distilled cherries), *framboise* (distilled raspberries), or *mirabelle* (distilled yellow plums). These will be discussed in the chapter on brandy. Confusion does arise because some English and French liqueurs are actually labeled "brandy" (cherry brandy, apricot brandy), although they are no such thing. In the United States they are more precisely labeled "cherry-flavored" or "apricot-flavored brandy," but since in both cases the products are alcohol flavored with fruit and sweetened they are technically liqueurs.

In Europe most firms use fresh or dried fruits to flavor the liqueur. In the US most firms use extracts or concentrates produced by specialists for flavoring cordials. These concentrates are in no way similar to chemical products with which some inferior liqueurs are flavored and which must by law carry on the label of the bottle the designation "artificial" or "imitation." Again both the generic and the proprietary brands are listed under the flavor headings.

Apricot

ABRICOTINE is one of the best-known apricot liqueurs and is produced by the firm of Garnier. The pulp and the fruit of the stone are macerated separately and then blended, which gives the liqueur a complex flavor of apricot and almond. Another proprietary brand is APRY produced by Marie Brizard.

Banana

CRÈME DE BANANE is a liqueur produced by macerating ripe

bananas, usually skin and all, in neutral alcohol, or else by using a concentrate of banana essence. It is a very sweet liqueur with what I personally find a cloying oily aroma. BANADRY is a brand of banana liqueur produced by Bardinet, much less sweet than the average banana liqueur.

Berries

Blackberries, blueberries, raspberries, strawberries all make pleasing liqueurs. The method of production is usually by maceration in neutral alcohol or brandy, and the better varieties are a subtle blend of different berry flavors supporting one dominant flavor.

CRÈME DE CASSIS is a rather special berry liqueur, the most famous version coming from the region of Dijon. It is flavored with black currants and produced at a relatively low proof. Its color is deep blue-purple. Diluted with four parts of cold white wine it becomes a Kir, named after the erstwhile mayor of Dijon, Cannon Kir.

Cherry

MARASCHINO is a cherry-flavored liqueur made from the Dalmatian marasca cherry. One of its first producers was an Italian, Girolamo Luxardo, whose firm is known the world over. Another well-known producer is Drioli. To make maraschino the cherry stones are distilled separately from the fruit. The fruit itself is first fermented. Ah, my attentive reader will say, is this not an *eau de vie*? No, oddly enough, for it is not the distillate that is used for this liqueur but the remaining pomace, or caked residue of the skins and pulp, which is then macerated in the distilled stone alcohol, after which the whole lot is distilled once more. It is then aged for at least three years and sweetened only before bottling.

PETER HEERING LIQUEUR, the famous Danish cherry liqueur, is a finely flavored liqueur, not too sweet and a lovely deep-red color. Most firms produce a cherry liqueur (and many, as I have said, insist on calling it a cherry brandy).

CHERISTOCK and CERASELLA are both brand names for cherry liqueurs produced in Italy.

Grapefruit

FORBIDDEN FRUIT is an American liqueur. It was originally made from the shaddock, a fruit very much like the grapefruit, which today often replaces it. It is made on either a brandy or a whiskey base.

Lemon
DOPPIO CEDRO is an Italian liqueur flavored with lemon, very sweet and sticky.

Tangerine
VAN DER HUM is a South African liqueur flavored with local tangerines which are macerated in South African brandy. Translated it means "What's his name," the exact name of its inventor having been forgotten.
MANDARINE NAPOLEON is a French liqueur flavored with tangerines, moderately sweet.

Sloeberry
SLOE GIN is a liqueur originally based on gin and flavored with the fruit of the sloeberry. (See also PRUNELLE under this heading in the section on seed liqueurs.) Today the liqueur is based on neutral alcohol and often blended with cherry-flavored alcohol. Its color is a vivid red and it can be used in small quantities in mixed drinks, especially gin fizz to turn it a striking color.

Orange
Orange liqueurs are flavored with the peel of the fruit which is distilled in neutral alcohol or brandy. The Dutch were the first to make this type of liqueur with oranges from Curaçao, their West Indian colony. The drink came to be known as CURAÇAO, a brandy-based amber liqueur, or TRIPLE SEC, a white curaçao.
COINTREAU, the best-selling orange liqueur, was originally made in France, but is now also produced in the US, Spain and Argentina. It is flavored with the peel of both bitter and sweet oranges.

AURUM is an Italian triple sec from the Abruzzi region, named by the Italian poet Gabriele D'Annunzio.

GRAND MARNIER is a very fine orange liqueur based on cognac. Bitter oranges from Haiti are macerated in new cognac for several months. The infusion is then distilled and the distillate is blended with herbs and sweetened. In Europe a less expensive variety not based on cognac is marketed under the label of Cordon Jaune.

The liqueurs so far have been either based on neutral alcohol or brandy. There are, however, a few based on the various types of whisk(e)y.

DRAMBUIE. This is a shortened rendering of the Gaelic *an dram buideach*, "the tot that satisfies." It is a liqueur from Scotland based on well-aged Scotch whisky, predominantly malt whisky. To this an essence of herb oils are added. The recipe was given to the Mackinon family by Bonnie Prince Charlie in 1746 while he was sheltering with them on the island of Skye after his defeat at Culloden.

GLENMIST is a Scotch-based liqueur flavored with herbs.

IRISH MIST is based on Irish whiskey. Its recipe follows that of the ancient honey and heather wines, which was somehow lost in the seventeenth century, then mysteriously returned by an Austrian to the Tullamore distillery in 1948. It is flavored with honey and herbs and has a very pleasing, subtle flavor of nuts.

IRISH VELVET is a blend of Jameson's Irish whiskey and Brazilian coffee, sweetened with sugar. Boiling water can be added to it, yielding instant Irish coffee, in which case fresh cream is floated on the top.

BAILEY'S IRISH CREAM is a liqueur based on Irish whiskey and containing fresh double cream flavored with chocolate essence.

ROCK 'N RYE is based on rye whiskey and sweetened with sugar. Some firms, including Leroux, flavor the liqueur with orange, lemon and cherries.

SOUTHERN COMFORT is a liqueur produced in St. Louis, Missouri. Based on bourbon, it is flavored with citrus fruits and peaches. It is only slightly sweet and is often drunk not as a liqueur but as a substitute for bourbon.

ODD MAN OUT

ADVOCAAT is indeed the odd man out, consistently defying all my attempts to classify it under any of the previous headings. Originally a Dutch liqueur, it is usually brandy-based and thickened with fresh eggs and sugar. The liqueur is very thick and very sweet. Some suggest wetting the liqueur glass with brandy (which also cuts out the sweetness) and then pouring in the advocaat—in this way it will not stick to the edges of the glass.

In Europe liqueurs are usually drunk as a *digestif* after a sumptuous meal. In America they were greatly in vogue during the 1920s when Prohibition bathtub gin was so obnoxious that its flavor had to be disguised somehow. A liqueur could also impart a flamboyant color to the cocktail, in tune with the spirit of the Roaring Twenties.

Femininity and liqueurs seem to go hand in hand—amazingly many a lady will happily sip a Black Russian while rejecting a straight vodka as altogether too potent. Whatever your convictions, enjoy!

RECIPES

Here are a few formulas for drinks made only with liqueurs:

GRASSHOPPER
$\frac{1}{3}$ *white crème de cacao*
$\frac{1}{3}$ *green crème de menthe*
$\frac{1}{3}$ *fresh double cream*
Shake well and serve in a tumbler.

MINT FRAPPE
Fill a cocktail glass with shaved ice and pour some crème de menthe over it.

PINK SQUIRREL
$\frac{1}{3}$ *white crème de cacao*
$\frac{1}{3}$ *crème de noyaux*

$\frac{1}{3}$ *fresh single cream*
Shake well and serve in a cocktail glass.

SNOWBALL
Pour about two tablespoons of advocaat into a tall glass and top with fizzy lemonade.

Liqueurs can also be combined with various spirits to make for some flavorful—and potent—concoctions. You will find recipes for the following drinks in the recipe section at the end of the appropriate chapter, as noted by the cross-reference. (The name in parentheses, of course, refers to the liqueur on which the drink is based.)

Alaska (yellow Chartreuse), *see* Gin
Alexander (crème de cacao), *see* Brandy
Black Russian (Kahlua), *see* Vodka
Bonnie Prince Charlie (Drambuie), *see* Brandy
Brandy Cocktail (Cointreau), *see* Brandy
Harvey Wallbanger (Galliano), *see* Vodka
Margarita (Cointreau), *see* Tequila
Rusty Nail (Drambuie) *see* Scotch whisky
Serpent's Tooth (Kümmel), *see* Irish whiskey
Shamrock (green Chartreuse and crème de menthe), *see* Irish whiskey
Sidecar (Cointreau), *see* Brandy
Stinger (white crème de menthe), *see* Brandy

LIQUEURS IN THE KITCHEN

Liqueurs also play a most important part in the kitchen. Here are a few cullinary uses.

Baking: Add two tablespoons of your favorite liqueur to the batter of any sponge cake.

Ice creams: Pour a measure of liqueur over vanilla ice cream. Coffee-flavored liqueurs are particularly good.

Soufflés: Add two tablespoons of liqueur to the egg and flour mixture before beating in the egg whites.

Fruit dishes: Pour a small glass of liqueur into a fruit salad. Especially good are the orange-flavored liqueurs. Try also pouring a small measure over a fruit flan.

Crêpes: Heat the crêpes in a chafing dish with butter. Add two tablespoons of liqueur (Grand Marnier is delicious for this recipe) and ignite, spooning the liqueur constantly over the crêpes to keep the flame burning.

A measure of liqueur will also enrichen any fruit dessert.

Brandy: The First Spirited Export

Brandy is distilled from wine or mash of fruit. It was probably the first spirit to be exported on a large scale. Throughout the Middle Ages the Dutch were carrying on a flourishing trade at the port of La Rochelle in France. They brought with them wood, salted fish and furs, and carried away the local salt, considered the finest in the world, and the local wine. As the art of distilling spread throughout the fourteenth and fifteenth centuries, the farmers experimented with their wines and discovered that a fine-flavored spirit could be obtained which was also economic to ship, as 9 barrels of wine could be condensed into 1 barrel of spirit. The French called it *eau de vie*, but the Dutch traders had another name for the distilled wine they were importing. They called it *brandewijn*, burnt wine, and from this the English came to call it *brandewine*, which was eventually shortened into brandy.

Today all wine-producing countries make some form of brandy—some for home consumption only, some for export. There is, however, one brandy outstanding in fame among all others and oddly enough it is the very brandy which the Dutch, Danes and English had been loading on their boats back in the seventeenth century at La Rochelle. It is called cognac.

COGNAC

As early as 1687 an advertisement in *The London Gazette* offered for sale "76 pieces of cognack brandy." (It is important to know that all cognac is brandy, but only the brandy from this small corner of the world is entitled to the world-famous name of cognac). There is a much quoted anecdote about the bishop of Angoulême who was introducing himself to a group of ecclesiastics. "Bishop of Engolisma in the Charente," he proclaimed. As this seemed to convey nothing at all to his peers, he added: "That means that I am the bishop of Cognac." Immediately their eyes lit up: "Cognac, Cognac! What a splendid bishopric."

Cognac is a protected word, and may only be used to describe the brandy produced in a strictly limited area of the Charente and the Charente Inférieur. The boundaries of the Cognac region were delimited in 1909 and they include seven *crus*, or areas, which form concentric circles around the heart of the region, the city of Cognac. Beginning from the center and working outward, the *crus* are: Grande Champagne, the Petite Champagne, the Borderies, the Fin Bois, the Bon Bois, the Bois Ordinaires

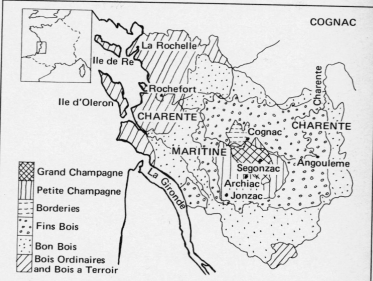

COGNAC

La Rochelle
Ile de Re
Rochefort
Ile d'Oleron
Charente
CHARENTE
Cognac
CHARENTE
MARITIME
Angouleme
Segonzac
Archiac
Jonzac
La Gironde

	Grand Champagne
	Petite Champagne
	Borderies
	Fins Bois
	Bon Bois
	Bois Ordinaires and Bois a Terroir

and the Bois à Terroir. Each zone produces a cognac of varying characteristics—a particular savor, a unique aroma, a different capacity for aging—all so valuable to the blender.

It should be noted that the designation *champagne* has nothing to do with the famous sparkling wine; rather, it is the French word for "field." The finest cognac of all is a Grande Champagne, and a very interesting Grande Champagne is Jean Fillioux produced by a family firm who own the estate of La Pouyade in the Grande Champagne area. They only use grapes from their own estate and therefore produce only a Grande Champagne cognac. In 1972 the Comité International d'Action Gastronomique et Touristique awarded the firm its "Cep d'Or" award for the high quality and individuality of their product. A Fine Champagne is a blend of at least 50 percent Grande Champagne with Petite Champagne.

Stars are another designation that may appear on a cognac bottle—usually three, although Salignac uses five. The stars signify that the shipper guarantees the quality of his product, usually indicating that the average age of the blended brandies is five years or more. Many shippers have stopped using stars on their label. Hennessy, for instance, maintains that its brand name is enough of a guarantee of quality; the firm calls their least expensive brandy Bras Armé, a name taken from the family crest which is a mailed arm and battle axe.

The letters VSOP on a cognac bottle stand for "Very Superior Old Pale"—"Very Superior" in that it is a cognac aged for at least four years but probably much longer; and "Old Pale," being a cognac light in color as distinct from the brown brandy popular in England in the eighteenth and nineteenth centuries and used for toddies and punches. Note that the letters on the bottle stand for English words though the product is French. This is partly because England was and still is one of the greatest importers of cognac: in 1973 the British drank over 20 million bottles. But also because many of the earliest families who established themselves in the trade in the eighteenth century came from England and Ireland: Richard Hennessy (1765) came from Cork, Jean Martell (1715) from Jersey, and Thomas Hine (1775) from Dorset.

A name often associated with cognac is Napoleon. There is a cognac which was presented to Napoleon in 1811 and subsequently imported to England, bearing the imperial N on its seal. This is not a commercial cognac but rather a collector's item and probably undrinkable. Cognacs labeled "Napoleon" are merely stressing in general terms the great age of their product.

Courvoisier cognac—"the brandy of Napoleon," as it asserts on the label—has a special story. After his abdication in 1815, Napoleon planned to escape to the United States. Two ships were loaded with all his belongings and among these was a large quantity of cognac supplied by Emmanuel Courvoisier. When the emperor abandoned his plan and gave himself up to the British, his luggage was transferred to two warships, the *Bellerophon* and the *Mirmidon*. The British officers were, of course, invited to sample his cognac, which became known as "The Emperor's Brandy" and thus, by extension, did Courvoisier come to be known as "The Brandy of Napoleon"! Today both their three-star and VSOP bottles carry these words and the well-known silhouette.

The spirit that the Charentais of the seventeenth century were distilling for their Dutch and English customers was very different from the cognac of today: it was aged very little and not blended. But it was distilled in exactly the same way.

The grape that is mostly used is the Ugni Blanc, a white grape locally called St. Emilion which produces a sourish white wine (not to be confused with the famous Bordeaux.) Two other grapes of some importance in the production of cognac are the Folle Blanche and Colombar.

BUREAU NATIONAL DU COGNAC

In October each farmer, or *viticulteur*, harvests his grapes with the help of itinerant workmen who in August had been picking the ripe red grapes in the Bordelais for claret, then the overripe white grapes for sauternes and who now through October and November are free to pick the late ripening St. Emilion grapes in the Charente.

The grapes are pressed in the old-fashioned horizontal press. The skins, pips and stalks go to a hydraulic press which gently presses out the remaining juice, without crushing the pips and stalks. The must then is transferred to the fermenting vats and converted into wine. Sulphur is never used in the production of cognac as it is in most wine-making processes. The white wine from which cognac is made is not matured. It is kept in sealed vats so that no air can reach it and as soon as it has fermented it is ready to be distilled.

Cognac is distilled twice in fairly small copper pot stills, designed on the principle of the apparatus used in the region in the seventeenth century. The stills are set over a

GILBEY VINTNERS

wood or coal furnace whose moderate heat brings the wine slowly to the boil. As the alcohol vapors are released, they collect in the head of the still, then are passed down through the neck, finally to condense in the spiral which is immersed in cold water. The first distillation produces a low wine called *brouillis*, of an alcoholic strength of about 28 percent. The *brouillis* is then redistilled. Between the two stills there is often a *chauffe vin*, where the heat of the distillate coming off the stills warms the wine as it enters the still, thus saving fuel. The product of the second distillation is known as the *bonne chauffe* and has an alcoholic strength of about 72 percent.

The distiller must use all his skill and experience during this second distillation to eliminate the imperfect first and last vapors and retain only the "heart" of the spirit. This operation is carried out slowly and with great

BUREAU NATIONAL DU COGNAC

Ground level chais *where the cognac lies maturing in oak casks for many years.*

BUREAU NATIONAL DU COGNAC

care under day and night supervision as the liquid condenses little by little from the still. The slow method of distillation and comparatively low strength at which the spirit is distilled allows the congeners from the wine to be retained in the distillate. This, combined with the long maturation in wood, produces a spirit of exquisite aroma and flavor.

When the cognac flows out of the condenser it is as white as gin. It must now be matured, for at least one year in the Cognac region by law. In practice it is usually left to mature for many years in the huge ground-level cellars called *chais*. The casks in which it is matured are made from the oak trees of the Limousin and Troncais forests. The wood of these oaks is very porous and their tannin soft.

Three substances may be added to cognac: sugar cane up to 2 percent of its volume; a minuscule amount of caramel to ensure consistency of color, and oak chips, which give the cognac more contact with the wood thus hastening its mellowing (too much, however, will give the spirit a woody taste).

Up to this stage the process of making cognac has been in the hands of the local farmers and small property owners, the *viticulteurs*. Now it passes into those of the big firms, the *négociants*, who will age and blend the cognac. It is they who hold the large stocks of maturing cognac and can afford the expensive business of blending, aging and shipping. Many of the small distillers have long-established links with the big houses and know what type of cognac they will be looking for. For instance, Delamain, who make a "pale and dry" cognac, require their suppliers to mature their cognacs in old casks from the beginning, whereas the general practice is to put a young cognac in a new cask where it will absorb more tannin and acquire a deeper hue. It is interesting to note that some of the best known firms, notably Courvoisier, own no vineyards at all and buy all their supplies of young cognac. Only the big firms can afford to maintain the huge reserve stocks of cognac necessary to produce a balanced blend. Every house has their *paradis*, where the very old cognac lies maturing, up to fifty years. After that it is thought that the spirit will deteriorate, so it is transferred to glass demijohns where it will no longer mature, as cognac only matures in wood. Hennessy claims to have the largest reserve of cognac in the world—100,000 hogsheads, enough brandy to fill 45 million bottles.

Aging is not only expensive because it ties up capital for such a long period; it is estimated that in the Cognac region the equivalent of 51 million bottles a year vanish into thin air through evaporation. This loss is philosophically known as the "angel's share." But the all-important aging of cognac cannot be speeded up. The raw, colorless young spirit must mature slowly in its oak cask, where the wood releases its tannin, giving the liquor an amber glow. At the same time a slow process of oxidation and evaporation takes place through the pores of the oak staves, developing the aroma of the spirit. The evaporation is redressed by topping up the casks with brandy from an earlier vintage. (This means, incidentally, there can be no such thing as a vintage cognac.) All commercial cognacs are blended, and this is the responsibility of the *maître de chais*, the master blender. It is he who selects cognacs of different *crus* and different ages, to combine the delicacy of one with the robust nature of another, the mellowness of a very old cognac with the fruity flavor of a younger one, and achieve by their mixture a perfect blend. This demanding job is a life-time vocation, often passed on from father to son. Martell's *maître de chais* is the seventh generation to work in the firm. He claims to be able to tell from the taste of a young cognac if there was anything wrong with the shape of the still. One *maître* summed up the skill of a good blender: *une très bonne mémoire*. He must be able to recall the qualities of each cognac he has ever tasted, and judge how well it will harmonize in his blend. When tasting, for a long time he only inhales the aroma, moving the cognac slowly around and around in the glass, and then to confirm his impression he takes a small sip. Once he selects the cognacs which will most enhance each other, they are thoroughly "married" in huge vats, then bottled.

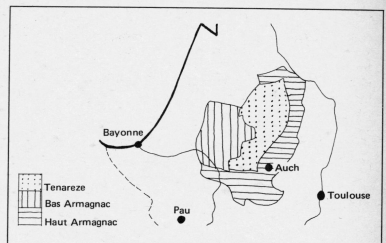

Tenareze
Bas Armagnac
Haut Armagnac

Bayonne
Auch
Toulouse
Pau

ARMAGNAC

Besides cognac, France produces another grape brandy of very high quality from the department of Gers in the southeast. This is the land of the Three Musketeers, and the brandy is called armagnac. Its production amounts to one-quarter that of cognac, and unlike cognac not very much of it is exported. The wine is made from the same grapes as those used for cognac, mainly the Folle Blanche which in this region is called Picquepoul. Unlike cognac, armagnac is distilled only once in a pot still, and is aged in black oak casks from the forest of Gascony. There are three exclusive production areas: Bas Armagnac, Tenareze and Haute Armagnac. A bottle carrying the simple description *armagnac* is often a blend of all three districts. *Hors d'Age* indicates that the armagnac is at least twenty-five years old. VSOP means that it is at least four years old. The traditional flat flask-shaped bottle in which armagnac is marketed is a copy of the Basquaise goatskin flask used by the local shepherds.

MARC

A third kind of brandy produced in France comes from the pomace of the wine press, the solid mass of skins, stems and pips which remain in the press after the grape juice has run off. This, mixed with water, is fermented into a rough alcoholic wash and then distilled to produce a type of brandy known as *marc*. It is pretty powerful stuff, the best being the *marcs* of Champagne and Burgundy.

EUROPEAN BRANDIES

Other brandies are produced throughout Europe: Spain produces a large amount of brandy, mainly in the Jerez district from the Jaen grape; Portugal, Germany, Italy and Greece all produce brandy, much of which is used for fortifying wines and in producing liqueurs. In Portugal, Germany, Italy and South Africa *bagaceira, tresterbrannt-wein, grappa* and *dop* brandy respectively are produced from the grape pomace (similar to the French *marc.*) From Greece comes Metaxa brandy and a special brandy from the island of Chios called *mastika*, which is flavored with resin.

NON-EUROPEAN BRANDIES

Non-European countries which produce brandy are South Africa, which exports to Scandinavia, Canada and West Africa; Australia, which produces a brandy made from the Doradillo grape, much of which is used for fortifying wines; and, in South America, mainly Peru and Chile. From Peru comes the pisco brandy distilled in the Ica district from muscat wine, matured in porous clay jars and bottled in curiously shaped statue bottles.

In the United States brandy for the most part is produced in California. At the end of the last century a fair amount of Californian brandy was exported to Europe to fill the gap in the market left by the dwindling cognac supplies after the phylloxera plague, but it was not really until after World War II that brandy was distilled in great quantities. It is now produced in column stills capable of turning out a thousand gallons of spirit per hour.

The principal grapes are the Thompson Seedless and Flame Tokay. Only brandies produced from 100% Californian-grown grapes can carry the word "Californian" on their label. The wine from these grapes is distilled in column stills, although some firms use a certain percentage of pot-distilled brandy in their blends. Brandy may be distilled at 170° US proof and must legally be aged

for at least two years. Unlike cognac, Californian brandy can either be a straight brandy or a blend.

Among the straight Californian brandies are the five-year-old and eight-year-old Ceremony, the ten-year-old Conti Royal, the eight- to eleven-year-old Old San Francisco Brandy and the six-year-old Royal Host. Among the blended brandies one of the finest is XO Rare Reserve produced by Christian Brothers, 50 percent of which is a pot-distilled brandy blended with an equal proportion of column-distilled brandy. Other blended versions include Aristocrat and Lejon brandies.

Many blended Californian brandies contain rectifying agents, sugar and flavoring substances which are added before bottling (but up to no more than 2.5 percent by volume). The principal flavoring matters are fruit extracts, fortified wines and the pod of the carob tree, also known as St. Johns bread, which gives the brandy a distinctive vanilla flavor. These brandies which are not matured for very long are the less expensive varieties, pleasant enough in long mixed drinks.

EAU DE VIE

So far we have only been concerned with brandies distilled from wine. As mentioned early on, brandy can also be distilled from a fruit mash; such spirits are known generically as *eaux de vie*. A distinction should be, but in practice is not, made between those beverages which have actually been distilled from the fermented juice of fruit and those in which a concentrate of fruit is added to a brandy base: cherry brandy, for instance, is not a true brandy as it falls into the latter category; KIRSCH or KIRSCHWASSER, on the other hand, is a true brandy as all the alcohol comes from the mash of cherries itself.

Eaux de vie are crystal clear and are never aged in wood as this would impair the lush perfume of the fruit which lingers in the distillate. Apples are fermented and distilled to give APPLE BRANDY, also known as EAU DE VIE DE CIDRE in France. There are, however, two special types of apple brandy, called APPLEJACK in the US and CALVADOS in France. Applejack claims to be America's oldest genuine distilled spirit, and it certainly played a central role in the lives of the early settlers. The Laird family, who now produce 95 percent of the applejack sold in the US, have records of applejack production going back to the 1690s. George Washington wrote to the family sometime prior to 1760 asking for their recipe, which was promptly supplied.

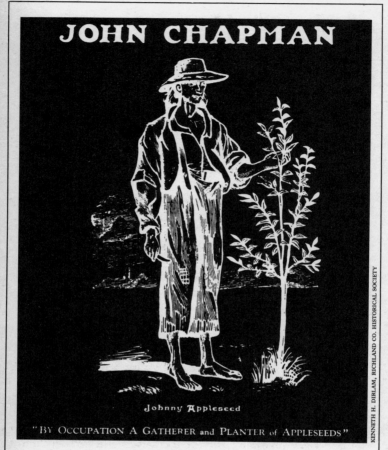

Johnny Appleseed

"BY OCCUPATION A GATHERER and PLANTER of APPLESEEDS"

KENNETH H. DIRLAM, RICHLAND CO. HISTORICAL SOCIETY

In 1828 an evangelist known as Johnny Appleseed was teaching religion along the Ohio River Valley. To his congregation he would hand out apple seeds, and when the trees bore fruit he taught them how to make applejack. A few years later it is recorded that Abraham Lincoln sold apple brandy in his Springfield tavern at 12 cents a half pint.

Applejack brandy is twice distilled in pot stills from cider and aged in charred oak barrels from four to eight years.

French CALVADOS hails from the town in Normandy at the center of the apple-producing area. Like applejack, it too is distilled twice in pot stills and aged in wood for about ten years. The people of Normandy have a special use for calvados: when they gorge themselves on a huge first and second course and feel the need to make room for more, they "bore a hole" in their stomachs, so to speak, by taking a gulp of fiery young calvados—a *trou normand*.

*A vine leaf infested by the insect
phylloxera and two enlarged views
of the insect.*

87

SLIVOVITZ, the national drink of the Balkans, is a brandy distilled from a mash of plums and aged in wood to give it a golden brown color. Plum brandy is also distilled in France from yellow plums and called MIRABELLE. In Alsace and Germany, it is called QUETSCH.

Eau de vie distilled from raspberries is called FRAMBOISE; from strawberries, FRAISE; from the Williams pear, POIRE. The latter is often attractively marketed with the fully grown pear inside the bottle. The bottles are hung on the branches of the tree over the flower and the fruit is allowed to grow and ripen in them. Apricot brandy is distilled in Hungary and called BARACK PALINKA. Most fruit brandies are distilled at a fairly low proof so that the flavor and the aroma of the fruit are carried over into the brandy.

Brandy was what the eighteenth-century gentry drank. To quote Dr. Johnson: Claret for boys—port for men—brandy for heroes. Its popularity carried right through into the nineteenth century. You will remember Dickens' Mr. Pickwick who invariably turned to brandy on any and every occasion. Many memoires and recollections of this time tell of the fair sex who laced their tea with brandy, a custom which my own grandmother indulged in while the rest of the family pretended not to notice. Gentlemen drank brandy and soda, and it was only at the turn of the century in the wake of the whisky boom that brandy was displaced. Winston Churchill recalled that: "My father could never have drunk whisky except when shooting on a moor or in some very dull chilly place. He lived in the age of brandy and soda."

The demise of brandy and soda at the end of the century was not only due to the development of blended whiskies from Scotland and the brilliant salesmanship which soon captured a worldwide market. In the 1860s the French vineyards were devastated by the plague of phylloxera well named *vastatrix*, an insect which destroys the vine by attacking its roots and leaves. In the 1880s the Cognac vineyards were attacked and the production of

cognac was almost brought to a standstill. Later it was discovered that the only remedy was to replant entirely the vineyards with French vines grafted onto American phylloxera-resistant stocks. Meanwhile, the cognac trade fell into disrepute for selling adulterated brandy. Until now cognac had been shipped in barrels and the shipper had no control over the bottling of his produce. After the 1890s it became the general custom to ship cognac in bottles labeled with the shipper's name. This practice was also boosted by the establishment in the mid-1850s of a glass factory in Cognac.

After a spectacular increase in sales after World War II (from 27 million bottles in 1947 to 112 million bottles in 1972), sales for 1973 and 1974 dropped to under 100 million bottles—partly because of the general trend towards "white" spirits like vodka and gin and partly because of the astronomical price of cognac. People are reverting to after-dinner port or to the less expensive brandies such as the German Asbach Uralt, which is becoming very popular. It has a very distinctive fragrant aroma and a dark golden color. Other pleasant brandies are the Italian Stock 84 Gran Riserva which is a strong, scented brandy, slightly on the sweet side, as is the Spanish Fundador, and the Italian Vecchia Romagna Etichetta Nera.

Fine old brandy should be drunk neat in a brandy glass, the stem of which can be slipped between the second and third finger allowing the glass to rest in the palm of the hand and gently warm the spirit thus releasing its wonderful aroma. This is one school of thought. Rémy Martin on the contrary maintain that the glass should be chilled to gather the full flavor of the bouquet. Whichever course you adopt, avoid the huge balloon glass, an ostentatious version of what a brandy glass should be. VSOPs or, if you are lucky, Fine Champagne and Grande Champagne are after-dinner drinks. Their lowlier brethren however, the three stars, are excellent mixers for soda, ginger ale and the like, and of course are the basis of many cocktails, some of which are listed below. Don't forget brandy in the kitchen for flavoring pâtés and stews, nor the fruit brandies for fruit cups, desserts and crêpes.

RECIPES

ALEXANDER
⅓ cognac
⅓ crème de cacao
⅓ fresh cream
Shake thoroughly and strain into a cocktail glass.

BONNIE PRINCE CHARLIE
1 brandy
½ Drambuie
1 fresh lemon juice
Shake well and strain into a cocktail glass.

BRANDY COCKTAIL
1½ cognac
1 Cointreau
1 tsp. sugar
2 dashes Angostura bitters
Shake well and strain into a cocktail glass.

SIDECAR
½ brandy
¼ fresh lemon juice
¼ Cointreau
Shake well and strain into a cocktail glass.

STINGER
2 brandy
1 white crème de menthe
Shake well and strain into a cocktail glass.

JACK ROSE
1 lemon juice
½ grenadine
2 apple jack
Shake well and strain into a cocktail glass.

Whisky, Whiskey or Uisge beatha?

U ISGE BEATHA is the Gaelic for *aqua vitae*, that water of life which the early distillers thought they had captured. It was in turn corrupted to *uiske* and thence to our modern form. Convention has it that Irish and American whiskey are spelled with an e, Scotch and other varieties produced throughout the world are spelled without it.

By legal definition Scotch whisky is distilled in Scotland and nowhere else, from malted barley with or without other cereals.

Irish whiskey is distilled in Ireland from malted barley and other cereals, often with a percentage of oats.

Bourbon whiskey is distilled in the United States and nowhere else, from a grain mash containing not less than 51 percent corn (maize).

Rye whiskey is not restricted geographically, being produced both in Canada (and spelled *without* the e) and in the United States, where it must be distilled from a mash of not less than 51 percent rye.

Other whiskies are distilled in different countries, principally Japan, Australia and Spain. Japanese whisky is primarily a blend ·of full-flavored whiskies produced locally in a pot still or imported from Scotland—Japan is by far the world's largest importer of bulk malt Scotch whisky—and lighter whiskies produced in patent or continuous stills. The mash for the latter is made of millet, corn and some rice. The whiskies are aged separately in charred oak casks and then blended.

All whisky is made from a fermented mash of any cereal grain but for the most part from malted barley, corn and rye.

SCOTCH WHISKY

For centuries farmers in Scotland have, during the winter months, distilled *uisge beatha* as a sideline to their farming. The necessary ingredients abound in the country: pure soft water from the burns, peat for fuel and fields of golden barley. At first, whisky was only produced for home consumption, with the side products of distilling— malt culms, draff and burnt ale—providing valuable cattle fodder for the winter.

Tradition has it that the art of distilling was brought to Scotland by the early Christian monks, some even say by St. Patrick. But another theory, about a primitive peasant, has been put forward by Neil Gunn, great whisky lover and expert, in his *Whisky and Scotland* (1935):

Peat, which is decomposed vegetable matter, is cut in April and May and left to dry throughout the summer before it can be burnt in the kilns.

JUSTERINI & BROOKS

Down round the southern corner of the *dun* there was a field of barley all ripened by the sun. . . . It was cut and harvested and a sheaf offered in thanksgiving; flailed and winnowed; until the ears of grain remained in a heap of pale gold: the bread of life.

In simple ways the grain was prepared and ground and set to ferment; the fermented liquor was then boiled, and as the steam came off it was by happy chance condensed against some cold surface.

And lo! this condensation of the steam from the greenish-yellow fermented gruel is clear as crystal. It is purer than any water from any well. When cold, it is colder to the fingers than ice.

A marvelous transformation. A perfect water. But in the mouth—what is this? The gums tingle, the throat burns, down in the belly fire passes and thence outwards to the fingertips, to the feet and finally to the head. . . .

Clearly it was not water he had drunk: *it was life.*

Whatever the origins of the art of distillation, the oldest written record which refers to the making of whisky comes from the Scottish Exchequer Rolls for 1494, which recorded "eight bolls of malt to Friar John Cor wherewith to make *aqua vitae*"—i.e., to distill. *Aqua vitae* in those days was used to denote any distilled spirit. Since Friar John was distilling his brew from malt (grain), he was in fact producing whisky.

Eight bolls of malt would produce a considerable quantity of whisky, and it can be charitably assumed that the monks of Friar John's monastery were dealing in a fair amount of local trade, just as their brother monk distillers were doing on the Continent.

Commercial production began in the eighteenth century, and the whole history of Scotch whisky is punctuated by the various attempts of many governments to tax it, not so much because they wanted to try and curb drunkenness (as was the case with the eighteenth-century gin act), but because it provided such a lovely lot of revenue. By 1725 Parliament had imposed a tax of sixpence on every bushel of malt that was fermented. As taxation rose, so did illicit distilling, especially in the remote Highlands. By the early nineteenth century one-half of Scotland's whisky production was coming from illicit stills, both in the Highlands and the Lowlands. In 1821 a Commission of Revenue inquiry was set up to investigate the problem, and two years later an act was passed reducing the duty on each gallon of whisky and stabilizing the license fee. George Smith of Glenlivet (The Glenlivet is today perhaps the most well-known of Highland malt whiskies) was the first distiller to take out a license and legalize his stills. This, his fellow distillers considered, was ratting, and, like Tom the Tinker's Men in the American Whiskey Rebellion, they attacked the licensed stills and actually managed to burn one down. But Smith was undaunted and merely saw to it that a pair of hair-trigger pistols were always in his belt. Soon the other distillers followed his example and illicit distilling gradually diminished.

In the first half of the nineteenth century, whisky was not a well-known drink; it was rarely drunk outside of Scotland. So little was the demand for the drink that most of the whisky sent to England at this time was redistilled and made into a colorless, tasteless spirit which was then flavored with juniper and sold to Londoners as their favorite tipple—gin. But in the 1860s, when the supply of brandy, the drink of the upper classes, was drastically reduced owing to the insect pest phylloxera which had ravaged the vineyards of France, the whisky producers in Scotland were quick to exploit the vacuum in the market.

Before following their adventures we should take a closer look at what they were selling.

Scotch whisky is the world's most prestigious and internationally enjoyed spirit. It is also a mystery. Like cognac, its distinctive flavor and bouquet simply cannot be reproduced anywhere else in the world. Some countries have even gone so far as to find supplies of water chemically similar to that of the famous Livet, importing Scottish barley, peat, and pot stills with no luck at all. Apparently their reckoning did not take into account the Scottish climate in which the whisky is matured—the soft clean air that permeates the cask and works on the young whisky to produce the unique liquor.

There are two types of Scotch whisky: malt whisky, made from malted barley and distilled in a pot still; and grain whisky, made from a fermented mash of corn (maize) and distilled in a patent or continuous still, also known as a Coffey still after the man who patented it in 1831.

When you ask for Scotch in a bar or restaurant, you will always get a blend of the two unless you are more specific. Malt whisky fans, however, will tell you that the only Scotch worthy of the name is a straight malt. Because of what it is made of, the way it is distilled and the long time it is allowed to mature, malt whisky is full-bodied, strongly flavored and expensive—three reasons why it is less popular then blended Scotch, especially in the United States where trends in taste veer to lighter, blander spirits in general and whisky in particular. To get some idea of this trend in consumption of blended versus malt whiskies it is only necessary to look at the 1975 Statistical Report of the Scotch Whisky Association. The US, which imports about half of all exported Scotch, imported 34.41 million proof gallons of blended Scotch as against 0.08 million proof gallons of malt whisky. It is interesting to note that of the ten major overseas markets, Italy imports by far and away the largest quantity of malt whisky: 0.14 million proof gallons, almost double that of the United States.

MALT WHISKY is made from malted barley *only* and is distilled twice in copper pot stills. All malt whisky is distilled according to a traditional process which involves five stages:

(1) *Malting the barley*: The first step is to induce the barley to germinate by soaking it in water. After the harvest, towards the beginning of October, the barley is brought to the distillery where it is thoroughly cleaned, dried and stored. The barley is then conveyed to the steeps where it is soaked in pure cold water for forty-eight hours or more, according to the judgment of the head maltman. As the barley begins to sprout, it produces two enzymes (organic substances which act as catalysts): cytase, which breaks down starch cells; and diastase, which converts moist starch into soluble sugar which in turn will be converted into alcohol during fermentation.

Traditionally the barley was taken from the steeps

*Turning the sprouting barley strewn on
the malting floor with the traditional
wooden skip.*

JUSTERINI & BROOKS

and spread on the floor of the malting house where it was regularly turned by the maltmen with their wooden skips in order to distribute the heat given off by the germinating barley. Today most distilleries use mechanical systems for this: either a rotating drum, or a Saladin box with a rotating fork which moves up and down the length of the box turning the sprouting barley over and over.

When the barley seed has grown roots and a shoot of the required length, germination is artificially stopped by drying the green malt (as it is now called) in kilns. A kiln is a kind of oven with a mesh floor on which the green malt is spread. Under the mesh burns a peat fire, and high above is a ventilator which draws the heat and smoke of the peat through the malted barley. The degree of smoke from the peat will eventually determine the more or less smoky flavor of the mature whisky. Today many distilleries buy their barley already malted from specialist malt producers and are most particular about the degree to which they require their barley to be smoked.

From the kiln the dried malt is processed through a range of malt hoppers to remove the rootlets and impurities, known as malt culms. The malt is then taken to the mill where it is coarsely ground.

(2) *Mashing*: In the second stage the ground malt, or grist, is conveyed to the mash tun, a huge vat with

The grist being poured into the mash
tun where the hot water will dissolve the
sugar in the malt.

97

perforated plates forming a false bottom. Here the grist is
mixed with hot water and thoroughly stirred, causing the
sugar in the malt to dissolve. The sugary liquid called
worts is drawn off through the false bottom, while the draff
or husks of barley left in the mash tun are processed and
used for cattle fodder. The worts are now cooled so as not
to kill the yeast which will be added to start fermentation.

(3) *Fermentation*: Under the control of the brewer
fermentation takes place in huge vessels of a capacity of
2,000 to 10,000 gallons called wash backs. Here a small
amount of yeast is added to the worts to promote
fermentation which takes place with much boiling and
bubbling as the enzymes in the yeast act upon the sugar to
produce carbon dioxide and alcohol. The seething liquid
was once controlled by men with birch sticks, but now is
kept in check by mechanical stirrers. After two or three
days, when fermentation is completed, the liquid—known
as wash and containing about $8\frac{1}{2}$ percent alcohol—is ready
to be distilled.

(4) *Distillation*: Malt whisky is distilled twice in two
copper pot stills. The first distillation takes place in the
wash still, the larger of the two. Heated by a coal fire or
steam-heated coils, the wash is brought to the boil. The
steam which is given off passes up the neck of the still and is
condensed in the worm (the coiled copper pipe which is
enclosed in a jacket of cold water).

This first distillate is called low wines and contains
about 17 percent alcohol. It is run into a spirit safe, a glass
box set in brass, so that the stillman can test the strength of
the spirit. If he judges this to be too low, distillation is

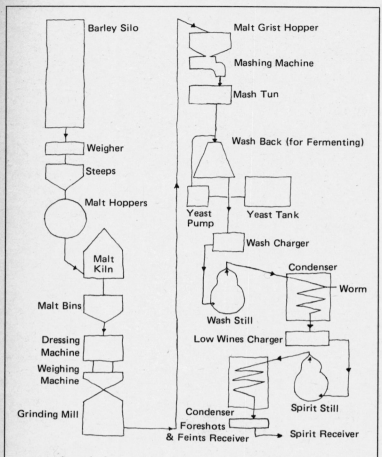

Barley Silo

Malt Grist Hopper

Mashing Machine

Mash Tun

Weigher

Steeps

Wash Back (for Fermenting)

Malt Hoppers

Yeast Pump

Yeast Tank

Malt Kiln

Wash Charger

Condenser

Worm

Malt Bins

Wash Still

Low Wines Charger

Dressing Machine

Weighing Machine

Condenser

Spirit Still

Grinding Mill

Foreshots & Feints Receiver

Spirit Receiver

stopped and the residue in the still, called burnt ale, is drawn off to be used as a fertilizer.

The low wines are now redistilled in the smaller of the two stills, the spirit still. The stillman will eliminate the first run of the distillation, the foreshots, which contain too large a proportion of impurities. The middle of the run is collected in the spirit receiver while the end of the run, the feints, are added to the foreshots and redistilled with the next batch of low wines. From the spirit receiver the whisky, now at a strength of about 115°–120° UK is run into the spirit store.

(5) *Maturation*: Years of maturation in casks are needed to make the rough and colorless newly distilled whisky into a smooth mellow drink. By law Scotch whisky must mature in wood for three years, but in practice good malt whiskies are matured for at least five years and sometimes for as long as fifteen years. Whisky is often matured in casks that have contained sherry. William

Saunderson, the blender of Vat 69, wrote: "It is well known that whisky stored in sherry casks soon aquires a mellow softness which it does not get when put into new casks; in fact the latter if not well seasoned will impart a woodiness much condemned by the practiced palate." Old bourbon casks are also used: this is because American law requires that bourbon be aged in new oak casks; as a result, in the past bourbon companies frequently sold their used casks to the Scotch whisky industry. The supply of these used casks may well dry up however, on account of the new American light whiskey which by law can be matured in used cooperage and which will presumably gobble up the used bourbon casks.

Whisky loses both strength and volume as it matures, both through evaporation and absorption by the wooden casks. This loss is called ullage and is calculated at about four million gallons a year which makes maturation a very expensive business.

There are four main types of malt according to where they are produced.

The Highland malt whiskies come from an area north of an imaginary line running from Dundee to Greenock. Among these are The Glenlivet, Glenmorangie and Glenfiddich, to name but a few. The center of the Highland distilling district is along the river Spey where there are more distilleries per square mile than in any other part of Scotland.

The Lowland malt whiskies are produced south of the same imaginary line. Most of these whiskies go for blending and only a very few are marketed as single malts.

The Islay malts come from the island so called and are very rich and peaty compared to the Highland malts.

Lastly the Campbeltown whiskies from the Mull of Kintyre. Only two of these are marketed as single malts:

Springbank, soft mellow and fragrant; and Glen Scotia, heavier with a strong peaty flavor.

GRAIN WHISKY, the other type of Scotch whisky is almost never drunk as a single whisky, but used largely for the purposes of blending. There is one single grain whisky on the market, Choice Old Cameron Brig. I have never tasted it, but some who have report that it is very sharp and almost metallic in flavor; others, however, maintain that it is quite pleasant. Grain whisky is made from a mixture of malted and unmalted barley and maize. The cereals undergo the same processes of mashing and fermentation described in the production of malt whisky, the unmalted cereals being cooked under steam pressure to burst the starch cells and allow the diastase from the malted barley to convert the starch into sugar. Being the product of the patent or continuous still, grain whisky contains a far smaller proportion of congeners than pot-distilled whisky and consequently does not need to mature in wood for such a long period of time. Unlike American neutral spirits that are distilled at 190° US proof and are therefore devoid of congeners, grain whisky distilled in Scotland is by law decreed to be a true Scotch whisky (and cannot be distilled at more than 166° UK); it is matured as such for three years in wood. Many distilleries market some of their malt whisky as a single or straight malt. The rest of the malts are sold to the blenders. The technique of blending Scotch whisky is, basically, achieving a balance between the strongly flavored, full-bodied malts and the lighter grain whisky, so as to produce a blend consistent in flavor and uniform in quality.

Before the middle of the nineteenth century little whisky was drunk outside Scotland, and that which was drunk was malt whisky. With the invention of the patent still in the 1830s and the beginning of an industry, the demand for a lighter (and cheaper) whisky was met by blending the grain whisky with malt whisky.

Blending was and still is done by each firm according to their own recipe, and few firms are willing to reveal the proportions of malt whisky to grain whisky in their blends. What they do like to reveal is the number of different malts that go into their blend—some boast of over thirty different types.

An important factor in a blend is the age of the malts. The age stated on any blended whisky label—for instance 8-year-old or 12-year-old—refers to the age of the youngest whisky in the blend, the others being very much older. The de luxe blends that many firms market presumably contain much older malts than the firms' ordinary blends.

Blenders work by their sense of smell. They "nose" the spirits to determine their qualities and then decide which ones and in which proportions they will be used. To blend the whisky, the casks of mature whiskies which the blender has selected are assembled and varying percentages of each are poured into a long trough which leads to the huge blending vats. Here the whiskies are thoroughly mixed by compressed air and are then set aside in casks to marry—that is, to allow the different whiskies to interact with one another. Some firms vat their malts before blending: that is, they blend all their malts together first before blending them with the grain whisky.

Blended whisky was introduced to the world towards the end of the last century by five big companies: Haig, Walker, Buchanan, Dewar and Mackie.

John Haig descended from a generation of farmer distillers. In 1824 he built a distillery at Cameron Bridge, and shortly after, he installed the newly invented patent or Coffey still in order to produce much greater quantities of cheaper whisky. By 1877 the distillery's output was in the region of 1,250,000 gallons of whisky per year. In that same year Haig joined with five other Lowland grain distillers to form the Distillers Company Limited. The DCL took over the Cameron Bridge distillery while Haig moved his blending business to Markinch, and in 1894 registered it as a limited company: John Haig and Co. Some years before this, his son had established a separate firm dealing principally with exports to the United States under the name of Haig & Haig and it is under this trade name that Haig whisky is sold in the United States.

At the turn of the century John Haig and Co. were appointed purveyors to the House of Lords—they had made it. Today they continue to carry on expanding their market to the tune of: "Don't be vague—ask for Haig."

John Walker and Sons Ltd. were created by John Walker—"Born 1820—still going strong." Johnnie set up as a grocer and wine and spirit merchant, steadily expanding his business and eventually promoting his son into partnership. Alexander Walker expanded the business still further by selling his whisky to the ships sailing from Glasgow. In 1880 he opened a London office and in turn took his sons into business with him. At the beginning of the century the firm started selling their whisky under the label designed by Tom Browne, the cartoonist: Johnnie Walker stepping out in his red coat, complete with top hat and monocle. Today he can boast of first place in world sales of Scotch whisky.

James Buchanan started his career as a whisky agent in London, and by 1884 he had acquired his own firm and began marketing Buchanan's Blend. He put his blend in a black bottle with a white label and proceeded to flog it by every form of salesmanship available. One day he went to a famous hotel in London's smart West End with a large party of guests. When they were seated, he ordered his own whisky. On being told that it was not available the entire party rose to leave, expressing their horror at the hotel being so poorly equipped. The next morning he received a large order for Buchanan's Blend. Like the next two nineteenth-century magnates we are going to discuss, Thomas Dewar and Peter Mackie (White Horse), James Buchanan was a self-made man who through hard work, business genius and amazing personality created for himself a worldwide fame in the Scotch whisky trade.

Buchanan's Blend was eventually supplied to the House of Commons, but the general public insisted on referring to it as "that black and white whisky," so that Black & White it became in 1904, with the well-known trademark of the black and white scotties.

John Dewar set up as a wine and spirits merchant in Perth and started blending his own whisky in the 1850s. He had the good idea of marketing his spirits in bottles while most of the other whisky merchants still sold theirs by the cask. When the flourishing business was inherited by two sons, the younger, Tommy Dewar, at once set off to try his luck in London town. On his arrival he succeeded in making himself thoroughly conspicuous at the annual Brewers' Show by drowning out all other business with his bagpipes. Orders began to flow in and soon Dewar's had a huge electric sign flaunting a Highlander in full regalia towering over the London skyline swilling his White Label, the Dewar blend. Both Dewar brothers received knighthoods and, having conquered the home market, set out to conquer the world. In 1892 Tommy made a two-year world tour and collected orders from twenty-six different countries. Today they hold second place in world sales.

White Horse Scotch whisky was blended by James Mackie & Co., who named their blend after the White

The original design for the figure of
JOHNNIE WALKER
BY THE LATE TOM BROWNE

Horse Cellar in Edinburgh, the inn from which the stage coach left for London. The full story is told on the back of every White Horse bottle. It was Peter Mackie who had realized the importance of a brand name at a time when so many whiskies were being sold unlabeled and he had the good business sense to latch onto the traditional inn with all its historical associations.

Like the other whisky barons, Peter was a larger-than-life character who loved dressing up in full Highland evening dress and brandishing outspoken political opinions, especially about Lloyd George. Oddly enough he was not particularly interested in advertising, and yet White Horse has been notorious in the field of promotion—from the early days of their campaign when they promoted their whisky as a medicine against influenza to their famous current slogan: "You can take a White Horse anywhere."

These are the "big five" of the Scotch whisky trade, and theirs were the names that signed the Scotch whisky announcement to the American people at the end of Prohibition (see p. 106). Now, together with John Haig, a founding member, they are all part of the DCL.

I can only mention a handful of the people and the stories behind the other two thousand odd blends of Scotch whisky: William Saunderson, who experimented in blends and finally made up a hundred or so and placed them in different numbered casks; he then invited some experienced whisky drinkers to come and pronounce their verdict and by general acclaim Vat 69 was chosen ... Giacomo Justerini, who came from Bologna in 1749 in the wake of a dazzling opera singer and eventually set up the famous firm of Justerini and Brooks who in 1919 launched J&B Rare ... Long John, named after the oversized proprietor of the Ben Nevis distillery ... Seagrams of Canada who bought and built distilleries in Scotland and

W. M. SAUNDERSON & SONS LTD

still blend their 100 Pipers and Chivas Regal, a high-selling
de luxe brand on the American market . . . Hiram Walker's
Ballantine and Old Smuggler . . . William Teacher, who at
nineteen had established his firm and at forty had eighteen
licensed retail premises where, with strict Victorian
morality (no smoking, no insobriety) he marketed his
Highland Cream . . . Cutty Sark, launched in 1923 and
owned by Berry Brothers and Rudd, one of the first very
light-colored Scotch whiskies; the label was designed by a
friend of Mr. Berry, a James McBey, showing the famous
sailing ship which is now a museum at Greenwich, the
swiftest in her day (note that Cutty Sark is called *Scots*
whisky. *Scots* or *Scottish* are in fact the correct adjectives
for most things hailing from Scotland, *Scotch* being only
permissible to qualify whisky and tape) . . . Arthur Bell &
Sons, William Grant & Sons . . . one could go on forever.
Instead let us go back in time and give the last word on
what is Scotch to the giant of the trade, the DCL.

In the 1850s Andrew Usher & Co. started vatting
their malt whiskies. This idea was soon followed by the
idea of blending malt whisky with the newcomer on the
market, grain whisky, produced in the patent still. As we
have seen blending was to be the big factor in boosting the
Scotch whisky trade, first in London then all over the
world. Of course the malt whisky distillers were not too
happy with this development and launched a firm
campaign against blends, claiming that they were not true
Scotch whisky. In 1905 the Borough Council of Islington

(London) took out a summons against two men who were selling blends as Scotch and contested that they were selling the product under false pretences since blends were not Scotch whisky. Judgment went against the defendants, whom the DCL immediately encouraged to appeal. The appeal was inconclusive and the grain distillers were as dismayed as the malt whisky distillers were jubilant. The DCL then requested that a commission from the Board of Trade be established to define once and for all what was whisky and what was not. The final report was published in 1909. It defined Scotch whisky as: "a spirit obtained by distillation from a mash of cereal grains saccharified [converted into sugar] by the diastase of malt." Triumph of triumphs, this definition included patent-still grain whisky since the mash always contains a certain amount of malted barley to convert the starch into maltose. The DCL had the last word, and Scotch is Scotch—malt or blended—provided it comes from Scotland.

Scotch Whisky

An Announcement

AMERICA is going wet: the Eighteenth Amendment is in process of being repealed. This immense revolution, which would have seemed incredible last December will in all probability have been accomplished before next December is out. We congratulate the Americans on the courage to admit that they made a mistake. We congratulate them also on the fact that they will again be able to get at a reasonable price and without danger of fraud and adulteration the best whisky that the world produces—Scotch Whisky.

But there may be some fear on this side of the Atlantic that the sudden increase of demand on the other side will have the effect of interfering with supplies here and that old customers may be neglected in favour of new. That fear can be dismissed. The signatories to this announcement—who share between them the greater part of the world's whisky sale—assure their British customers that their reserves, amounting to millions of gallons, are sufficient to meet the requirements of whisky drinkers all the world over and that the distilleries under their control are capable of replacing them as they are drawn on.

This means that not only now, but as long as whisky is drunk, there will be ample supplies, fully aged and matured, of the famous blends whose names are, and always will be, a guarantee of the highest quality.

JOHN DEWAR & SONS LTD., Perth, London and Liverpool
(White Label)

JOHN WALKER & SONS LTD., Kilmarnock and London
(Johnny Walker)

JAMES BUCHANAN & CO. LTD., London and Glasgow
(Black & White)

JOHN HAIG & CO. LTD. (owning HAIG & HAIG LTD.),
Markinch, Scotland and London
(Haig)

Distillers
WHITE HORSE LTD., Glasgow and London
(White Horse)

There is no purer drink than Scotch Whisky. It is the purified essence of malted barley, and was called by the early distillers *Usquebaugh*, which means the Water of Life. It is enjoyable; it is healthful; it places no strain on the digestion; it is an excellent tonic. It is recognised as one of the major amenities of civilisation.

WHITE HORSE DISTILLERIES

RECIPES

"There are two things that a Highlander likes naked and one of them is malt whisky."

—Old Saying

How is Scotch drunk?—Naked, or with a little pure water. Blended Scotch, on the other hand, is often drunk with a variety of mixes, from soda water to fizzy lemonade.

Here are a few well-known drinks based on Scotch whisky:

ATHOLL BROSE
1½ Scotch whisky
1 tbs. clear honey
2 tbs. fresh cream
Warm a glass, pour in the honey then the cream, add the whisky and mix well.

HET PINT
4 pints ale
½ pint whisky
3 eggs
1 tsp. nutmeg
4 oz. sugar
Heat the ale and nutmeg in a pan and add sugar. Add beaten eggs and whisky. This is a traditional drink for Hogmanay, the Scots New Year.

ROB ROY
½ Scotch whisky
½ sweet vermouth
Shake well and serve in cocktail glass.

RUSTY NAIL
⅔ Scotch whisky
⅓ Drambuie
Stir well and serve on the rocks.

WHISKY SOUR (can also be made with bourbon)
1 Scotch whisky
½ tsp. sugar
1 tsp. egg white
¼ fresh lemon juice
Shake well and strain into a cocktail glass.

THE MANSELL COLLECTION

IRISH WHISKEY

Irish whiskey is supposed to be the oldest in the world. It is first mentioned in the *Book of Leinster* as *uisge beatha*, the Celtic rendering of *aqua vitae* which was the medieval name for distilled spirits. As in Scotland, whiskey was first produced in Ireland by the monks, chiefly for curative purposes, but by the fifteenth century it had become a cottage industry, with everyone distilling it for home consumption.

In the following century an act was passed requiring distillers to hold a license from the Lord Deputy. A nice exception was made for peers, gentlemen owning property valued at over £10.00 and borough freemen who could happily continue to distill without a license.

In the seventeenth century whiskey was taxed at four pence a gallon and the illicit stills trebled. These distilled (and still do distill) potheen, the Irish name for the illicit spirit. A nineteenth-century traveler in Ireland came across an illicit still and left a thorough description of what he found: apparently he entered a small thatched cabin in which a semicircle of stones surrounded a huge peat fire; resting on the stones was a 40-gallon tin vessel which both served to heat the water for mashing the barley and provided the main body of the still. The mash tun was made up of a cask with an outlet at the bottom, and a layer of heather and oak husks filtered the wort, which was then fermented in another cask and afterwards distilled in the tin vessel to which a neck and worm had been connected. In the traveler's estimation, the spirit thus distilled was highly flavored with peat and very fiery. Commenting on the latter quality, a sixteenth-century visitor noted: "The Irish eat raw meat which boyleth in their stomachs with the *aqua vitae* which they swill."

Irish whiskey dominated the English market in the last century before the blended Scotch boom. The legal product was more mellow than the Highland malt whisky because their pot stills were larger and they distilled the liquor three times. Apart from this the method of production is similar to that of Scotch malts.

The Irish distilleries grew up around the ports so as to be able to buy grain at competitive prices. But in these locations they had to contend with imports: wine and brandy for the wealthy, rum for the rest. Towards the end of the eighteenth century two famous firms were established in Dublin: John Jameson & Son founded in 1780, and John Power & Son founded in 1791.

The Jameson family originally came from Scotland and married into a family of Bow Street distillers. In 1780 John Jameson became the owner of the Bow Street distillery while his younger brother acquired a distillery at Fairfield. (The younger brother is of interest only because his daughter Anne married Giuseppe Marconi, father of the great inventor.)

Jameson did much to encourage the Irish farmers to grow top-quality barley for his distillery, and much to encourage foreign trade. He became a personal friend of Theodore Roosevelt and did much business in America. To begin with, the whiskey was shipped in casks, but after the invention of the patent still and the ensuing competition with the less expensive Scotch blends Jameson started bottling his product to ensure that only his top-quality product was sold under his label.

John Power had, as far as equipment and business policy went, one of the most advanced distilleries in the early nineteenth century. The company was using the latest inventions, including an internal telephone, and was one of the first to open a lunch hall for its employees. The production of whiskey, however, followed the age-old

traditions: the malt was ground by millstones up till the time that the last miller retired (not so long ago), and only then was a power hammer installed. Distilling was a seasonal event coinciding with the harvest, which meant that the labor force was needed at the distillery in the winter months but not in the summer. John Power resolved this problem by employing river fishermen from Wexford: they worked in the Dublin distillery in winter and returned to their fishing in the summer. In the 1890s a village was built at Clygate by the firm for the men of Wexford to inhabit while they were at work at the distillery.

John Power and Son proudly and steadfastly kept to the traditional pot-still method of distillation until 1953, when they introduced a patent still and started marketing blended Irish whiskey in addition to their long-established malt whiskey; gin and vodka were added as well.

From Northern Ireland comes one of the finest Irish whiskies—Old Bushmills. *Uisge beatha* was distilled at Bushmills in the early Middle Ages and was consumed in great quantities by warriors going off to battle. It was one of the earliest whiskeys to be exported to America where it was deservedly popular.

Like Scotch malt whisky, Irish whiskey is usually drunk neat or with a little water.

RECIPES

IRISH COFFEE
1 tsp. sugar
2 Irish whiskey
Top up with strong black coffee and cover with fresh cream.

SERPENT'S TOOTH
1 Irish whiskey
2 sweet vermouth
½ fresh lemon juice
½ Kümmel
Dash of Angostura bitters
Stir well and strain into a cocktail glass.

SHAMROCK
1 Irish whiskey
1 dry vermouth
Dash of green Chartreuse
Dash of crème de menthe
Stir well and serve in a cocktail glass.

THE OLD CROW DISTILLERY COMPANY

AMERICAN WHISKEY

Whiskey was distilled in the Colonies from the early eighteenth century onwards, mainly by that wave of Scottish farmers who moved westward into Maryland and Pennsylvania, and who brought with them an age-long tradition of distilling part of their annual cereal crops.

Rye was the main crop, and after the harvest, the farmers would take a certain portion to distill into whiskey for home consumption. Soon, however, distilling became a major part of the economy. As trade and commerce opened up, these farmers started to send their rye to the Eastern markets, by way of a packhorse. But the journey was long and the grain often spoiled before it reached the market; and added to this was the fact that a horse could only manage four bushels of rye. If, however, the farmer distilled his grain into whiskey a horse could carry the equivalent of twenty-four bushels on his back and the merchandise actually improved in transit. Whiskey became their principal export and by 1790 over 5,000 distilleries were operating on a commercial basis in Pennsylvania alone. Whiskey also became legal tender: 25 cents or more a gallon, according to quality.

Of course it was not long before this commodity attracted the ever-eager eye of the Treasury. In 1791 its secretary, Alexander Hamilton, imposed the first tax of the newly formed US government on the production of whiskey: 60 cents a gallon on the capacity of every still and 90 cents per gallon on each gallon produced.

The indignation, not to mention the resentment and the anger of the Western farmers was naturally fierce, especially since the government demanded to be paid in hard cash, not even in whiskey. And needless to say, the person who bore the brunt of their resentment was the tax collector. In Lexington the people made an effigy of

Colonel Thomas Marshall, chief collector for the district, and held a public hanging. Robert Johnson, tax collector for Allegheny fared even worse: he was physically attacked, tarred and feathered, and had his horse stolen. The situation was obviously getting out of hand, and it was particularly serious for the young government as it called into question its fundamental right to impose taxes on a federal basis.

The insurgents were therefore labeled rebels and their cause became known as the Whiskey Rebellion. In 1794 George Washington gathered together the incredible number of 15,000 militiamen, a larger army than any that fought in the Revolutionary War, and under the command of General Henry Lee, governor of Virginia, they set forth to face the motley crew of rebel farmers. The most colorful part of his army were the lads from Jersey who marched to the tune of:

> *To arms once more, our hero cries*
> *Sedition lives, and order dies*
> *To peace and ease then bid adieu*
> *And dash to the mountains, Jersey Blue.*

The dour rebel farmers had another name for these dashing soldiers—"the watermelon boys." This is what they published in an article against their fellow citizens:

Brothers, you must not think you frighten us with . . .
infantry, cavalry and artillery composed of your
watermelon armies from the Jersey shores. They
would cut a much better figure warring with the crabs
and oysters about the Cape of Delaware.

As far as battles go, the whole campaign was nothing
more than a storm in a teacup. Finding virtually no
resistance, the government army arrested a few leaders and
left a garrison to keep an eye on things through the autumn.
But politically, it was a definite triumph: the right to levy
federal tax had been established, and even more important
the right to call in federal troops from one state of the
Union to enforce law in another.

While all this upheaval was going on, between 1791
and 1794, an ever-increasing exodus of farmers poured out
of Pennsylvania and down the Ohio into Virginia and
Kentucky: not so much because they hoped to avoid tax
there, but because they were fed up with being harassed: on
the one side by the government if they did not pay tax;
and on the other side by Tom the Tinker's boys, as a
faction of the rebels were called, who went about riddling
with bullets the stills of those who did pay the hated tax.

In Kentucky they planted their traditional crop of rye
but soon found out, as the earlier settlers had before them,
that the land was more suited to corn and distilling corn

whiskey. They had also experimented in blending corn and rye distillates—in other words, bourbon. Popular tradition has it that the father of bourbon whiskey is the Reverend Elijah Craig, a Baptist minister: the story goes that it was he who discovered the right proportions for the blend and the fact that it aged best in charred oak casks.

But whatever the reverend's accomplishments, bourbon was not properly called by that name until a later date—when the Pennsylvania emigrants who had previously called their rye distillate Monongahela, after a river in the area, decided to name their corn whiskey after their new home, Bourbon County.

On account of the influx of farmers from Pennsylvania in the 1790s, Kentucky soon became one of the largest distilling areas in the land, and by 1810 over two thousand distilleries were in operation with an annual output of about two million gallons. Today 70 percent of all spirit production in the US takes place in Kentucky.

The 1791 excise tax was only the first instance of the federal government's ever-increasing interest in spirit taxation. In 1862 the tax was 20 cents a gallon. It soon shot up to 63 cents, and by 1864, it had hit $1.50 a gallon. Moonshining, of course, rocketed and the government wisely lowered the tax. But it quickly began to creep up again, and today the figure is an astronomical $10.50 per gallon, and of course moonshining still thrives: it is estimated that illegal distilling equals 25 percent of legal produce.

American whiskey can be straight or blended. A straight whiskey is the product of a single distillery,

*Grain crusher where the kernels of
grain are crunched to the right
consistency before going into the cookers.*

115

SCHENLEY DISTILLERS INC.

distilled at a proof not exceeding 160° US. It is aged in new charred oak barrels for at least two years and then reduced in proof to no lower than 80° US for bottling. Since it is distilled at this relatively low proof, it is a whiskey rich in flavor.

No one quite knows how or when the tradition of charring barrels originated. It probably happened accidentally and it was discovered that the aging liquor became more mellow when the barrels were charred.

Bourbon is the most popular straight whiskey in America. In the production of bourbon the grain mash must contain at least 51% corn, the remaining ingredients being a combination of rye and malted barley (collectively referred to as small grains). Each distiller selects his own formula for his own particular type of bourbon. The most popular proportion is around 60% corn, 28% rye and 12% malted barley. Since rye and malted barley produce a more strongly flavored distillate than corn, a formula with a greater proportion of small grains will produce a more flavorsome bourbon. James Beam's grain bill, for instance, contains 75% corn, 13% rye and 12% malted barley.

All the grain is carefully selected for top quality and delivered to the storage department. It is then coarsely ground and weighed into the proper quantities to be fed into the cookers. The grains are handled separately as rye

cooks much faster than corn. Corn is often cooked in pressure cookers, a procedure which many distillers consider damaging for rye. Cooking breaks down the starch cells in the grains, and when they have been sufficiently cooked (in boiling water, continually agitated to avoid scorching) the temperature is reduced to about 140°F. Now the malted barley is added to convert the starch into sugar. The mash is further cooled to about 70°–75°F, and then the yeast is added and fermentation begins. The process lasts from three to four days, after which the fermented mash (known as distiller's beer) is stored in the beer well until it is taken to the stills.

American whiskey is fermented by one of two possible methods: sour mash (used mainly in the production of bourbon) and sweet mash. In the sweet mash process fresh yeast is added to the mash and the mixture is allowed to ferment for about thirty-six to fifty hours. In the sour mash process, one-third of the spent beer from a previous fermentation is added to the fermenting vat containing the fresh mash and fresh yeast. This sour mash then ferments for a much longer period—anything up to ninety hours. The sour mash process does not of course result in a sour-tasting whiskey. On the contrary the distillers who practice it maintain that their whiskey has a finer flavor precisely because of the longer fermenting period.

Some distillers use a modified version of the traditional pot still to distill their whiskey, usually redistilling the first distillate. The process is known as doubling. Other distillers use a continuous still, but never distill over 160° US (except in the case of light whiskey.) The stillage—that is, the residue of the mash from which the alcohol has been distilled—goes to be processed into animal feeds, while the distillate goes either to the high wines room or to the cistern room. In the former, certain types of blending occur which are not permitted in the cistern room. The whiskey that goes directly to the cistern room is diluted with water to reduce it to about 100° US. It is then matured in new charred white oak barrels.

After maturation the whiskey goes to the blending department. In the case of straight whiskey, the whiskey is brought down to the correct bottling proof by the addition of water and then it is filtered. No coloring is added. In the case of blends, the straight whiskeys are added to the neutral spirits or grain whiskey according to each blender's recipe. Color is standardized by the addition of caramel. The blend is then filtered and bottled.

A blended straight bourbon is the product of several distilleries and distillations. It corresponds to a blended or vatted malt whisky in the Scotch whisky trade.

Plain blended whiskey, on the other hand, is a blend of not less than 20 percent straight whiskey whether rye or bourbon, with the remaining 80 percent being composed of other whiskeys or neutral spirits. Like the malts in a Scotch whisky blend, the blender selects his straight whiskeys to give aroma and flavor; he chooses the neutral spirits to make the blend lighter in body and smoother. As many as seventy-five different straight whiskeys will go into making a good blended brand. The exact composition—that is the percentage of aged whiskey or whiskeys and the proportion of neutral spirits—must be stated on the back label on all bottles of blended whiskey.

An odd man out in the American whiskey bunch is Tennessee whiskey. Jack Daniel's Tennessee Sour Mash whiskey, to name just one, is technically not a bourbon. Although it is made in the same way, it is filtered through charcoal before bottling, and this changes its designation.

This is how they do it at the Hollow: felled when the sap is down, the hard maple trees are cut in strips and stacked into ricks. They are then set on fire and hosed at intervals so that the residue, instead of being ash, is pure, hard maple charcoal. This is then granulated and poured into room-high vats in the warehouse. Slowly the whiskey filters through the charcoal and the taster checks it for "sippin' smoothness," the whole batch being rejected if it is not found to be so. Jack Daniel's is certainly in demand: from 930,000 cases in 1971, by 1975 it had increased its sales to 1,275,000 cases.

One last word: the term "bottled-in-bond." This is not a separate type of whiskey but merely an identification that the whiskey is at least four years old, bottled at 100° US proof, produced in a single distillery (for a straight whiskey), and is the product of a single year and season. The bottled-in-bond designation is in itself no guarantee of quality, but in fact most distillers choose only their best whiskies for this bottling.

RECIPES

HIGHBALL
(Railway men in St. Louis in the 1880s used a ball on a high pole to signal the engineer to speed up. It was called a highball. This is a drink meant to be gulped down.)
2 whiskey
Pour over ice into a tall glass and top with soda.

MANHATTAN
(When Henry Hudson sailed into New York Bay he found some Delaware Indians on a certain island. They had a ball and the Indians thereafter referred to the island as "Manahachto-niek," the island where we all got drunk.)

1 bourbon
½ dry vermouth
½ sweet vermouth
Dash of Angostura bitters
Stir and strain into a cocktail glass.

MINT JULEP
4 sprigs of mint
1 lump of sugar
1 tbs. water
2 bourbon
Place mint, sugar and water and ice in a tall glass and top with bourbon—an unrefined version.

OLD FASHIONED
1½ bourbon
1 tsp. sugar
3 dashes Angostura bitters
Mix in a tumbler with ice.

CANADIAN WHISKY

Another whisky of world fame is Canadian whisky. Before the 1920s there was little Canadian whisky on the market as the distilleries had been closed down by the government all through World War I. In 1926 the Canadian Distiller's Corporation Ltd. entered in a joint venture with the Distillers Company Ltd. of Great Britain. Two years later they acquired the controlling shares of Joseph E. Seagram and Sons—which had been established in 1857, ten years before Canada became a nation—and formed the Distillers Corporation—Seagram's Ltd. Today Seagram's V.O. is the largest selling Canadian whisky in the world.

RECIPES

CANADA COCKTAIL
1½ oz. Canadian whisky
2 dashes of Cointreau
2 dashes of Angostura bitters
Sugar
Shake and strain into a cocktail glass.

RYE AND DRY
2 oz. Canadian whisky
Pour over ice in a tumbler and top with dry ginger ale.

Gin, alias

Mother's Ruin

GIN is a spirit produced from a very pure grain or cane spirit flavored with juniper. It is from the juniper berry that gin gets its name. The French for juniper is *genièvre*, the Dutch *jenever*, and from an amalgam of the two the word was anglicized and shortened to gin.

The gin story starts in Holland. For a long time it had been known that the juniper berry had diuretic properties, relieving bladder and kidney complaints as well as gout and rheumatic pains. So it was that in the middle of the sixteenth century, Dr. Franciscus de la Boe, also known as Sylvius, a professor of medicine at the University of Leyden, began mixing his *aqua vitae*, or distilled spirits, with the juice of the juniper berry in an attempt to find a new cure-all. But soon—as was the case with liqueurs, which originated as herbal medicines made by medieval apothecaries—the medicine became a popular drink because of its pleasing taste and the appealing effects of the alcohol.

The first commercial distiller to make use of Dr. Sylvius' medicine was Lucius Bols, who ran a distillery at Schiedam. He started producing gin in about 1575. (Dutch gin, incidentally, is often called Hollands after its country of origin, or Schiedam after Bols' native town, which has become the largest center of gin distillation in Holland.)

Gin grew in popularity and quickly came to be much appreciated in army circles as a well-known purveyor of Dutch courage. The English soldiers too, fighting in the Netherlands under Sir Philip Sidney, acquired a taste for the spirit and brought it back home. Soon London, Portsmouth, Plymouth and Bristol began their own distilling.

In the early part of the seventeenth century in England the consumption of gin was more or less restricted to the ports: beer, ale and cider were still the main drink of the people; wine and brandy that of the richer classes. But in 1688, James II lost his throne and fled to France. William of Orange, a Dutchman, became king of England with his consort queen Mary. One of his earliest acts was to ban the importation of wine and spirits from the enemy France and to encourage distillation from home-grown grain. Every Englishman was given the right to distill spirits from home-grown grain and the consumption of gin rocketed. From 500,000 gallons consumed in 1690, it rose to 5,000,000 in the 1720s and to 18,000,000 gallons twenty years later. The gin era was on.

By 1736 drunkenness and social disorder had become so rampant that a Gin Act was introduced to limit production and sales. The taxes on distillation were raised and the sale of gin in quantities under two gallons was forbidden. The people, however, were not about to be done out of their accustomed pleasure. The act was ignored, illicit distillation flourished and the product was merely given a different name to avoid the law. It was cheekily called "Parliamentary Brandy," or else "Ladies' Delight," "Cuckold's Comfort," or "Last Shift." There was little control over the quality of this gin and some pretty hair-raising spirits must have been bootlegged at this time.

The jails were bursting with offenders against the Gin Act, although juries often found it difficult to convict them as witnesses and informers mysteriously disappeared or were found beaten, maimed or dead. A certain Captain Dudley Bradstreet, who had been an informer, noticed that: "Most of the gaols are full on account of this act, and it occurred to me to venture on the trade." So the informer turned bootlegger and started up a kind of coin-op in Blue Anchor Alley. He set up a billboard with a picture of a large cat under whose paw a lead pipe was inserted. "When my house was ready for business I inquired what distiller in London was most famous for good gin and was assured by several that it was Mr. Langdale in Holborn. When the liquor was properly disposed I got a person to inform a few of the mob that gin would be sold by the cat at my window next day provided they put money in his mouth from whence there was a hole that conveyed it to me . . . at last I heard the chink of money and a comfortable voice say Puss, give me two pennyworth of gin. Instantly I put my mouth to the tube and bid them receive it from the pipe under her paw and then measured and poured it into the funnel from whence they soon received it. After this manner I went on for a month in which time I cleared upwards of two and twenty pounds."

It would be interesting to know who this "most famous" distiller of good gin was, this Mr. Langdale from Holborn. For it was at this time when Captain Bradstreet was writing his memoirs (published in 1775) that some of the great London gin distilleries were establishing themselves. Booth's founded their distillery at Clerkenwell in 1740 and Mr. Alexander Gordon established himself in Clerkenwell ("the well of the clerks"), which had become the center of the gin distilling business due to the purity of

the well water, an essential ingredient in the manufacture of gin.

The spirit was to be had everywhere. It was sold by apothecaries and barbers, by tobacconists and many merchants, who offered it to their clients over a business transaction. It was hawked in the streets and sold in the jails where William Smith, an early prison reformer, counted in 1776 "no less than 30 gin shops at one time in the King's Bench, and I have been credibly informed by very attentive observers that upwards of two hogshead or 120 gallons of gin which they call by various names, as vinegar, gossip, crank, mexico, skyblue etc. were sold weekly. . . ."

The social evils of this excess have been made famous by Hogarth's print *Gin Lane* in which you can see the horrors it created in eighteenth-century urban life. Gin provided the cheapest way out of a miserable existence. The inscription over the door of the gin shop (at the left of the print) reads:

Drunk for a Penny
Dead drunk for twopence
Clean straw for Nothing

The novelist Smollet tells that "they lay until they recovered some of their faculties, and then they had recourse to the same mischievous potion." And Lord Harvey wrote: "Drunkenness of the common people was so universal by the retailing of a liquor called Gin, with which they could get drunk for a groat, that the whole town of London and many towns in the country swarmed with drunken people from morning to night, and were more like a scene from a Bacchanal than the residence of a civil society." To go back to the Hogarth print: the only members of the community who are doing any business, and they are prosperous, are S. Gripe (who runs the pawn shop) and the undertaker. Mr. Gripe is taking in a carpenter's coat and saw, the very tool of his trade, without which he will not be able to support himself, and behind him a housewife waits to pledge her saucepan, kettle and fire tongs. In front of the pawnbroker's shop an old man and a mangy dog share a bone, and an itinerant gin-and-ballad seller sits on the steps. These ballad sellers would wander up and down the streets promising a free glass of gin to anyone who would buy their poems. This one has sold most of his clothes (which is why gin was often called "strip-me-naked"). Nearby a mother feeds her baby on gin. But the most appalling figure is the mother who has dropped her child as she drunkenly reaches for more snuff.

Towards the end of the eighteenth century more acts were passed to check the consumption of gin, all to little avail. A further attempt to impose controls was the Beerhouse Act of 1830, which allowed beer to be sold without a license. Gin distillers were quick to realize that they would have to offer some advantage to gin drinkers if they were to compete with the new beer sales. They started to look for more attractive premises in which to sell their liquor, and thus gradually were the dreary and shabby public houses of the previous century converted into the resplendent edifices known as gin palaces. Charles Dickens gives a vivid description of one of these palaces in his *Sketches by Boz*, illustrated by George Cruikshank: "the gay building with a fantastically ornamental parapet, the illuminated clock, the plate-glass windows surrounded by stucco rosettes and its profusion of gas lights in the richly gilt burners, is perfectly dazzling when contrasted with the darkness and dirt we have just left."

These "dazzling" gin palaces were the poor man's refuge from urban squalor, and gin the panacea for his wretchedness. Gin was not the only spirit sold in these palaces but it was certainly the most popular, so much so that Prime Minister Gladstone in 1874 could claim that he had been borne down in a torrent of *gin* when his tentative bill to restrict the sale of alcohol in general cost him an election.

Gin was popular but not yet fashionable. Soon the advent of the cocktail and other factors were to change its social status, but before tracing the social climb of this low-class spirit to the dizzy heights of the Dry Martini I refer you back to Cruickshank's sketch to see what type of gin was on the market in the 1850s and what it became in the second half of the century.

Cruikshank shows the gin stored in huge vats and called by a variety of quaint names. Dickens tells us that: "ingenuity is exhausted in devising titles for the different

descriptions of gin; and the dram-drinker portion of the community . . . are left in a state of pleasing hesitation between 'The Cream of the Valley,' 'Out and Out,' 'The No Mistake.' '' This variety of "brands" of gin would have depended on the ingredient added to give the spirit a kick—additives such as oil of turpentine or sulphuric acid, quite common in these times, and always a great quantity of sugar to mitigate the pungent spirit. The barrel on the right, Old Tom, is the most interesting for us as Old Tom is still on the market today, produced by the firm of Boord and Son in London. It is an old-fashioned sweet gin, the closest we can get to the eighteenth century.

Although gin orginated in Holland, by the time Boord's was in business London had become the capital of the world, exporting far and wide. Boord's Old Tom, with its label featuring a cat and barrel, was to be found both in the Far East, where the famous trademark was synonymous to gin, and in America where Boord's had to fight several law suites to protect their brand from local products.

In the 1850s the London distillers started to market a new type of gin, unsweetened gin, which eventually became known as London dry gin. The prestige of London distilled gin has never waned, and although dry gin is now produced the world over, gin distilled in London is still considered the finest: Beefeater, for example, the largest-selling imported gin in the United States, with their famous trademark of the Tower's Tudor guard, symbol of London; and Tanqueray, who bottle their gin in an imitation of a London fireplug.

What promoted the change from sweet gin to dry gin is not clear. It could have been the beginning of a general trend in taste away from the heavy-bodied spirits towards lighter, smoother flavors (which is what happened in the Scotch whisky trade at the end of the century when the lighter, blended versions of Scotch captured the market). Another factor may have been the invention of the patent or continuous still in the 1830s. With the new still, a highly purified neutral spirit was being produced so that the gin distillers would no longer have needed to mitigate their gin with quantities of sugar.

The demand for dry gin greatly increased at the turn of the century when cocktails became the vogue in fashionable circles. The dry variety blended well in a mixture, whereas the highly flavored sweet gin would tend to dominate the cocktail.

The word *cocktail* dates back to the beginning of the nineteenth century. How the name came to be applied to a form of drink is uncertain, and theories abound. To me the ones that appear the most likely are those that maintain that *cocktail* denotes a mixture: for example, a mixed drink came to be called a cocktail because in horse circles a horse of mixed blood had its tail bobbed and was known as a cocked tail. If you don't like that one, try this: at cock fights it was customary to toast the winning bird with a mixed drink containing as many ingredients as there were feathers left in his tail.

The ingredients of early cocktails are a far cry from what we would choose today, for at this early stage the cocktail was associated with the idea of a tonic or *digestif* and usually contained medicinal bitters. An American journal in 1806 described a cocktail as a "*stimulating* liquor, composed of spirits of any sort, sugar, water and bitters" (my italics). In mid-century Mark Twain, writing to his wife from London, also described the cocktail as a *digestif*. There is little to marvel at in the recipe he gives, but his choice of a surrounding in which to imbibe it is a bit quaint: "Livy my darling, I want you to be sure to have in the bathroom when I arrive, a bottle of Scotch whisky, a lemon, some crushed sugar and a bottle of Angostura bitters. Ever since I have been in London I have taken in a wine glass what is called a cocktail (made with these ingredients) before breakfast, before dinner and just before going to bed. . . . To it I attribute the fact that up to this day my digestion has been wonderful . . . simply perfect."

In the British Far Eastern colonies the colonels and

their staff were mixing their medicinal quinine tonic water with gin. In like style the Royal Navy were mixing their medicinal bitters with gin, dubbing the mixture a pink gin. Whether or not these combinations were called cocktails, they certainly contributed to the fashion for mixing and to the sales of dry gin as a most versatile mixer.

Whatever its etymological history, the fashion for cocktails grew steadily—from the early bottled ones taken as a refreshment on shooting parties and other outdoor events to the incredible mixtures concocted in speak-easies during Prohibition when *anything* was used to disguise the nauseous taste of bathtub gin.

The cocktail created an era of its own, the Cocktail Age, when cocktail parties assumed a social importance they were never to relinquish, especially in the United States. The monarch of this era which extended through the 1920s and '30s was the Dry Martini, and fanatical devotees spread its cult throughout the States and Europe. According to John Doxat, author of *The Book of Drinking*, the Dry Martini got its name from its originator Martini di Arma di Taggia, bartender at the Knickerbocker Hotel in New York City during the first decade of this century. The drink was not in fact first associated with Martini Dry Vermouth from Italy but was made with Noilly Prat, dry gin and orange bitters. Today the bitters are discarded and frequently the famous Italian vermouth, coincidentally synonymous, replaces the French.

Endless are the recipes for mixing a Dry Martini, almost as endless as the Martini *bons mots*—"I can't wait to get out of these wet clothes and into a Dry Martini"—and the jokes—the henpecked businessman addressing the world at large after a chilly reception from his wife: "I've only had tee Martoonis and I'm not so much under the affluence of incohol as some thinkle peep."

Another cocktail of an earlier vintage was the John Collins, named after its London originator:

My name is John Collins, headwaiter at Limmer's,
  Corner of Conduit Street, Hanover Square.
My chief occupation is filling the brimmers
  For all the young gentlemen frequenters there.

When instead of dry gin the brimmers were filled with Old Tom, the drink was called a Tom Collins.

With the advent of dry gin and the blossoming of the cocktail age, gin became as socially acceptable as brandy or

DISTILLERS COMPANY LTD.

whisky for both men and women. (The popular sweet gin,
however, virtually disappeared.) Today there are basically
two types of gin on the market: Dutch gin and dry gin.

Dutch gin is distilled in a pot still from malted barley
and rye at a comparatively low proof, and the resulting
maltwine is distilled again with juniper berries and other
botanicals according to each firm's secret recipe. The low
proof at which it is distilled allows a considerable portion of
congeners from the grain mash to pass over into the
distillate. This results in a gin which is full-bodied with a
pronounced malty flavor. (I tend to attribute an oily
quality to it, but this could be because I accompany it with a
snack of Amsterdam smoked eel.) Similar to Dutch gin are
the various schnapps distilled in most northern European
countries and the German gin marketed under the name of
Steinhager.

Dry gin is produced by distilling a very pure spirit
with junipers and other botanicals. The base spirit which
the gin distiller uses is distilled from a mash of grain;
sometimes cane spirit is used. It is distilled at a high proof
in a patent still which eliminates the congeners, resulting in
a pure, tasteless and odorless spirit. The flavor in the gin is
added by redistilling this base spirit with botanicals:

Gilbey's gin distillery at Harlow built in 1963 to house the hundred-year-old stills moved from the old distillery.

GILBEY'S LTD.

juniper berries, coriander seeds, angelica root, calamus root, cassia bark, lemon and orange peel, licorice and cinnamon. As for the proportions and varieties of botanicals used, each firm has its own jealously guarded secret recipe, but normally about 5 pounds of botanicals are used per 100 gallons of spirit. These flavoring agents are either suspended in a mesh in the head of the still over the spirit which, when heated, vaporizes and passes through the botanicals, capturing their aroma, or they are actually steeped in the spirit which is then vaporized and condensed into gin. The stillman must determine which part of the distillate he will use. The first part, or heads, is discarded and collected in a feints receiver. The stillman with his long experience and keen sense of smell noses the gin and samples it for strength. When he judges that what is coming from the condenser is top-quality spirit, he switches the flow and directs it into the gin receiver. The end of the still run, or tails, is also discarded and run into the feints receiver. The gin is then mixed in huge vats and reduced in strength by the addition of water to bottling strength. In England this is 70° UK proof for the home market and 83° UK proof for export, except for Gordon's gin which is bottled at 83° UK proof. Being a spirit without congeners, gin does not need to be matured but is piped directly into the bottling hall.

How is gin drunk? The fishmongers in London's Billingsgate market used to drink it diluted with milk! Dutch gin and the schnapps varieties are drunk neat, chilled, in tall glasses. Dry gin is rarely drunk neat except in the gin trade where it is drunk diluted with a little water. A pink gin is virtually a neat gin with only a dash of Angostura bitters added. Plymouth gin, slightly more aromatic than most dry gins, is often drunk as a pink gin.

Based on gin is the well-known bottled Pimms No. 1 Cup. Its other ingredients are a secret, so closely guarded that on joining the firm every employee signs a pledge never to reveal the recipe if it is ever discovered by him. Pimms is a really delightful summer drink, reminiscent of large brimmed hats and croquet lawns. It is drunk diluted with fizzy lemonade and garnished with lemon and cucumber peel, borage and mint, served in tall glasses with lots of ice.

Tonic water is probably the most favored mixer for long drinks and then there is the plethora of cocktails based on gin. Here are a few of the best known.

RECIPES

ALASKA
¾ dry gin
¼ yellow Chartreuse
Shake well and strain into a cocktail glass.

BRONX
½ dry gin
¼ sweet vermouth
¼ dry vermouth
Juice of ¼ of an orange
Shake well and strain into a cocktail glass.

DRY MARTINI
2 dry gin
¼ dry vermouth
Stir well and strain into a cocktail glass, add a squeeze of lemon rind or an olive. (No two Martini fans will ever agree on ingredients, proportions or method.)

GIBSON
Same as a Dry Martini, but with a cocktail onion in it.

GIMLET
½ dry gin
½ Rose's lime juice
Shake well and strain into a cocktail glass.

GIN FIZZ
1 dry gin
Juice of ½ a lemon
¼ tbs. sugar
Shake well, strain into a tall glass and top with soda water.

GIN RICKEY
2 dry gin
Juice of 1 fresh lime
Dash of gomme (syrup)
Pour over ½ a fresh lime and ice cubes in a tumbler and top with soda.

GIN SLING
2 dry gin
Juice of 1 lemon
1 tsp. sugar
Dash of Angostura bitters
Pour over ice cubes in a tumbler and top with water.

ORANGE BLOSSOM
½ dry gin
½ fresh orange juice
Shake well and strain into a cocktail glass.

WHITE LADY
½ dry gin
Juice of ½ a lemon
¼ Cointreau
1 tbs. egg white
Shake well and strain into a cocktail glass.

Rum: The Rebel Spirit

RUM is distilled wherever the sugar cane grows, principally in the West Indies where Christopher Columbus is said to have planted the first cane cuttings on his second voyage. A seventeenth-century manuscript describing the Island of Barbadoes [sic] tells that: "the chief fuddling they make in the island is rum bullion, alias kill-devil, and this is made from sugar cane distilled, a hot, hellish, and terrible liquor." Some rums continue to be distilled in this way—from the juice of the sugar cane itself—but most rum today is distilled from fermented molasses, the residue of sugar manufacturing.

By the middle of the seventeenth century, molasses were being exported to New England and rum distilleries were in operation, first in Boston and then in other ports of Massachusetts and Rhode Island. Throughout the colonial era rum was the moving spirit, both socially and commercially. It became the main form of currency in what was called the Triangular Trade. The three points of this trade route were the West Indies, New England and the Gold Coast of Africa. The West Indies needed slaves to work on their sugar plantations; New England needed molasses from the West Indies to make the rum which they then traded with the African chiefs for more slaves. The rum that was not used in this triangle of bartering was exported to England to pay for imported manufactured goods.

In 1733 the British Parliament issued the Molasses Act, heavily taxing molasses imported to New England from the French and Spanish West Indies in order to restrict trade to their own colonies. The New Englanders ignored the act and embarked upon a career of rum smuggling and general defiance of British imperialism which finally culminated in the Revolution. (Rum, it seems, was forever becoming associated with various breeds of outlaws: first the buccaneers and pirates, then these pre-revolutionary daredevils; and even in the twentieth century, when it lent its name to a further crop—the "Rum Runners," who during Prohibition, smuggled in rum and other spirits from "Rum Row," which floated just outside the limit of US territorial waters.)

Not only was rum a major factor in early American commercial life—it was a prime social necessity. As we have seen, in the early nineteenth century, spirits were still considered a necessity, not a luxury as they are today. They kept one healthy and fit to work. In Portland, Maine, for

MARY EVANS PICTURE LIBRARY

instance, the city hall bell was officially rung at 11 A.M. and 4
P.M. to announce to the workmen the beginning of their
rum break—at the boss's expense, of course.

The colonial tavern was the center of community life
and many an evening was passed by the fireplace over a
Yard of Flannel—rum, cider, spices, eggs and cream—or
over a flip. For the latter, loggerheads were kept in the
fireplace to be plunged red hot into the mug of rum and
beer. (The expression "to be at
loggerheads" came into being
around this time—recalling
moments when the fiery irons
were used not in a flip but about
the head!)

THE MANSELL COLLECTION

Rum soon became a popular
drink in England and France, as
well as in the Colonies. It was
especially familiar in British
Royal Navy circles where, from
the middle of the seventeenth century, it was issued neat as a
daily ration. Later on Admiral Vernon (Old Grog to his
sailors because of his long grogram coat) broke with
tradition. He had the rum diluted with water and this drink
eventually came to be called a grog.

Because of the differences in methods of production,
climate and water supplies, the rum produced in the
various islands of the Caribbean differ among themselves
in color and flavor. Rum can, however, be loosely classified
into two types: the light-bodied, light-looking and very
dry rums such as those of Cuba and Puerto Rico, and the

Cutting the sugar cane in Puerto Rico.

ECONOMIC DEVELOPMENT ADMINISTRATION COMMONWEALTH OF PUERTO RICO

heavy-bodied, pungent dark rums from Jamaica. This classification is traditional only and not really exact, as today each of these countries produce both types of rum.

The traditional rum was a full-bodied, richly flavored spirit, the product of the pot still. With the invention of the continuous still and the fashionable trend toward lighter-bodied spirits, light rum began to gain popularity.

Whether distillation is carried out in the pot still for heavy rum, or in the continuous still for lighter rum, production starts with the sugar cane. After the harvest the canes are taken to the sugar mills where heavy rollers crush the canes to extract the juice. Once the juice has been boiled down to a thick heavy syrup, it is pumped into centrifugal machines which crystallize the sugar and separate it from its residue, the molasses.

The molasses are then diluted with water and fermented with yeast. When the yeast has used up all the sugar it dies, and the wash (appropriately called the dead wash) is ready for distillation. As much as 150 pounds of dead yeast cells collect at the bottom of a 24,000 gallon fermenting vat.

The light-type rum is fermented relatively briefly for about one day, while the heavy-type rum is fermented from anywhere up to twelve days which allows a larger proportion of congeners to develop. In Jamaica the dunder, or skimmings, from the previous distillation are added to the wash.

BACARDI LTD.

The wash is then distilled either in a pot still at a low proof to produce a heavy, flavorsome spirit, or in a patent, or continuous, still at high proof to produce a light spirit. In the first case only the middle run of the distillation, the *madilla*, is used; as in the production of whisky and cognac, the heads and tails are redistilled in a subsequent distillation.

The distilled rum must next be matured. Like whisky the pot-distilled rums will have to mature for much longer, anything up to twenty years: the continuous-still rums for much less. Like all distilled spirits just after they have been distilled, rum is colorless, but it acquires a certain hue as it matures in wood. It then either has caramel added to it according to the color desired, as does the Bacardi brand of dark rum known as Carta Oro (gold label)—or it is filtered through charcoal to remove all trace of color, as is Bacardi's Carta Blanca (silver label) variety.

Jamaican rums, as we have said, are traditionally pot-distilled—heavy, pungent and dark. Today most Jamaican rums, for instance Appleton's, are blends of pot- and continuous-distilled rums. Much Jamaican rum is shipped in bulk to England and matured there.

Contrasting with these are the light-bodied Cuban rums (no longer exported to the West) and Puerto Rican rums. The latter is dominated by the Bacardi brand who produce a light-colored dry rum; a dark-colored dry rum; a "151" high proof rum which they recommend for gourmet cooking; and Añejo, a blend of rums all aged for six years and over.

The Barbados rums are distilled in both pot and continuous stills and are medium heavy; the rums from Haiti are distilled not from molasses but from the juice of the sugar cane in pot stills and are fairly light-bodied. In Guyana where the sugar canes grow along the Demerara River, Demerara rums such as Lamb's Navy are produced. Lastly there are the rums from Martinique, mainly exported to France, which are often made from cane juice syrup, like Rhum St. James, or from molasses, like Rhum Negrita.

A certain amount of rum in still made in New England, heavy, dark and pungent. In most rum-producing areas a raw spirit is distilled from lower-grade molasses and sold locally under the name of TAFIA. Java produces a rum called BATAVIAN ARAK which is dry and has a high aromatic flavor.

Rum is sometimes drunk diluted with hot or cold water. Personally I prefer it when spiced or flavored with mixers.

RECIPES

CUBA LIBRE
2 light rum
1 tbs. lime juice
Pour over ice in a tall glass and top with Coca-Cola.

PLANTER'S PUNCH
2 dark rum
1 lemon juice
1 tsp. grenadine
Dash of Angostura bitters
Pour over ice in a tall glass and top with soda water.

DAIQUIRI
1 Bacardi light rum
½ lime juice
¼ grenadine (or less, according to required sweetness)
Shake well and strain into a tall glass.

TRADER VIC'S PUNCH
1¼ light rum
1½ dark rum
Juice of ½ orange
Juice of ½ lemon
A slice of pineapple
1 tsp. sugar
Dash of grenadine
Mix well over ice in a tall glass.

Some hot drinks for a cold winter's night:

HOT BUTTERED RUM
1 dark rum
1 lump sugar
½ tsp. of butter
A few cloves
Place ingredients in a mug and top with boiling water.

HOT TODDY
1 dark rum
1 tsp. of sugar
Twist of lemon peel
Place ingredients in a mug and top with boiling water.

TOM & JERRY
1 dark rum
1 tbs. egg yolk and egg white (beaten separately and then combined)
1 tsp. sugar
Place ingredients in a mug, top with boiling water and sprinkle with nutmeg.

Vodka:
The Meteor
Spirit

VODKA has been distilled in Russia, Poland and Czechoslovakia since about the twelfth century. It is made from a neutral spirit which is then further purified by seeping it through charcoal to remove all traces of aroma and flavor. Popular fantasy has it that it was traditionally distilled from potatoes but this is just not the case. Like brandy (*aqua vitae, eau de vie*) and whisky (*uisge beatha*) vodka too was once called the water of life: *zhinznennia voda*. Gradually the word *voda* was changed to the affectionate diminutive *vodka*, "the dear, little water." Like other European spirits it was mostly used as a medicine, and the rough spirit would have been flavored with herbs, berries and spices as many Eastern European vodkas are today.

From being a medicine, vodka soon became the staff of life. *The Russian Primary Chronicle* of the Middle Ages, giving an account of Russia's conversion to Christianity, explains that Prince Vladimir of Kiev rejected the offer of an embassy of abstaining Muslims to convert his people to Islam because: "Russians are merrier drinking—without it they cannot live." Drinking was indeed a national pastime. Vodka was sold in government-licensed shops called *kabaks*, which unlike Western taverns dispensed no food. A man went to a *kabak* to do a spell of solid drinking and hopefully to reach a state of alcoholic stupor—*zapoi*—which might last several days. Easter was the great time for drinking, after the long and tedious cold spell and before the rigors of another agricultural year.

Towards the end of the eighteenth century, methods of distillation improved and vodka was being further purified by filtering through charcoal. In 1818 a Russian by the name of Pierre Smirnoff opened a distillery in Moscow and by 1886 was purveyor to the royal household of the czars. At the end of the century the sale of spirits was the largest single item of revenue on the imperial budget.

Distillation was banned in Russia during World War I and continued to be so after the October Revolution of 1917. The ban was only lifted in 1925 in an attempt to curb illicit distillation. In the meantime, Vladimir Smirnoff, a descendant of Pierre, was living in exile in Paris where he met a fellow Russian named Rudolph Kunett, a naturalized American citizen. To him Vladimir gave the right to the name Smirnoff and to the production of Smirnoff vodka in the USA. In 1934, just after Prohibition was repealed, Kunett began producing Smirnoff vodka from a small distillery in Bethel, Connecticut, trading on the

prestige of the Russian name and the Imperial eagles. The enterprise was a commercial failure, and in 1939 Kunett sold out to Hublein.

Between 1939 and the mid-1940s the sales of vodka were so minimal that the spirit was not even listed by the US government as a separate spirit, but categorized under Miscellaneous (as tequila still is today, although it may well become another meteor in the spirit trade). Harold Grossman in the latest edition of his guide to wines, spirits and beers wrote: "When this book first appeared in 1940, it was unthinkable that a separate chapter should be required on Vodka. In the short space of three decades the most neutral of spirits has risen ... to a degree of popularity in America that ranks it second only to Bourbon and Blended Whiskey and Scotch."

The spark that ignited the vodka comet was a California fad. There is in Los Angeles a restaurant called the Cock 'n Bull Tavern, and the proprietor of this tavern, Jack Morgan, had brought back with him from England a taste for ginger beer. He started producing the stuff but found it had little appeal. Stuck with quantities of ginger beer, he started experimenting with various spirits to make a cocktail and came up with the Moscow Mule—ginger beer and Smirnoff vodka.

Vodka soon became the craze throughout the States and by 1961 vodka production reached more than

NOVOSTI PRESS AGENCY

19,360,000 gallons per year—a twenty-fold increase in ten years. Smirnoff vodka still heads the world market sales of vodka.

Vodka is made from neutral alcohol, which is distilled mainly from a mash of grain. Many brands specify on their labels that the spirit has been distilled from 100% grain spirit. Corn and rye are used in the United States, corn and malt barley in England. Some brands, however, use cane spirit for, according to US law, vodka can be distilled from any material provided that it is at or above 190° US proof, so as to be without flavor or aroma (in contrast to whiskey, for example, which is distilled at a low proof to retain the flavoring congeners).

However, distillation—even at this high a proof—does not completely eliminate all the congeners. One way to further purify the spirit is to filter it through charcoal. Other secret processes for eliminating all flavor and odor have been patented—Gordon's claim to have "a patent on smoothness" (No. 2,879,165) for unique screening, every drop of vodka being screened fifteen times by a hush-hush agent, making it "cleaner than the purest mountain air."

Of course this type of vodka is not aged. But in Russia and Poland (where there is less of a premium on tastelessness), vodka is often flavored and aged in wood. Starka vodka, from Russia, is pale amber in color, having been aged for up to ten years in wine casks. Okhotnichya, also from Russia, is a vodka flavored with many herbs, while Pertsovka vodka is highly spiced with capsicum peppers and cayenne. Zubrowka vodka comes from Poland and is flavored by a sprig of grass which only grows in eastern Poland to feed a special breed of bison; the bison appears on the label and the grass actually comes inside the bottle, giving the vodka a yellowish tinge and an aromatic flavor. In Finland, too, a popular brand of vodka is associated with an animal, this time a white reindeer: translated the name means "the spirit of white reindeer." (Everyone knows, so the ads say, that when you see the sun, the moon and a white reindeer all at the same time, you can make a wish and it will always come true.)

Traditionally vodka is drunk ice cold, neat, at one gulp with savory tid-bits to help it on its way. Flavorless vodkas, of course, are wonderful mixers, especially with fruit juices.

RECIPES

BLACK RUSSIAN
1 *vodka*
½ *Kahlua*
Pour over ice cubes in a tumbler and stir.

BLOODY MARY
2 vodka
3 tomato juice
Juice of ½ a lemon
2 dashes Worcestershire sauce
Salt & pepper
Shake well and strain into a tall glass.

BULL SHOT
1 vodka
3 clear beef bouillon
Pour over ice in a tumbler.

HARVEY WALLBANGER
1 vodka
3 orange juice
¼ Galliano
Pour over ice cubes in a tall glass floating liqueur on top.

MOSCOW MULE
1 vodka
Juice of ½ a lime
Pour over ice cubes in a tumbler and top with ginger beer.

SCREWDRIVER
1½ vodka
1 orange juice
Shake and strain over ice in a cocktail glass.

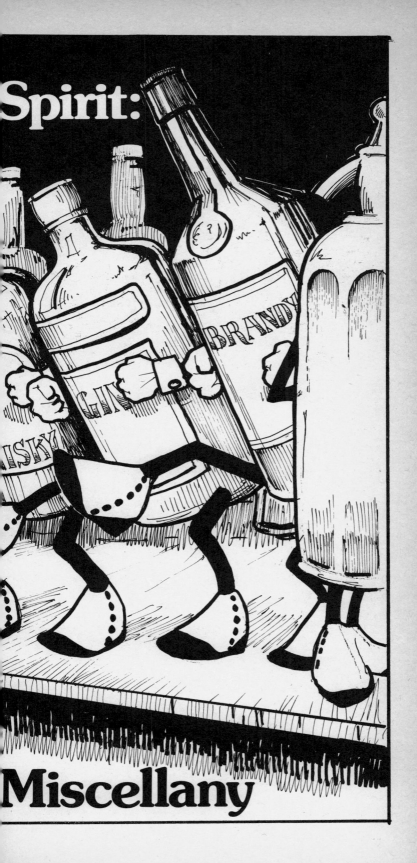

BESIDES the five big international spirits surveyed in the previous chapters, there are a few others of more or less regional importance.

MISCELLANY

AQUAVIT or AKAVIT (sometimes called *schnapps* in Holland and Germany) is the national beverage of the Scandinavian countries. It is distilled in column stills from grain or potatoes and flavored with caraway seed. It is traditionally drunk neat, ice cold, in one gulp. There are many brands of *aquavit* in Sweden and Denmark, some drier than others such as ODAKRA TAFFEL AQUAVIT and SKANE AQUAVIT. Norway produces a LINIE AQUAVIT which is sent across the Equator to Australia and back, to let it mature during the sea voyage.

ARAK is a spirit distilled in the Far East from a variety of ingredients such as fermented palm sap, dates and coconut milk. Batavian arak is distilled in Indonesia from molasses.

OKOLEHAO is a spirit distilled in Hawaii from the roots of the Ti plant. It has a strange fruity flavor and is drunk either neat or in a cocktail.

PASTIS is a French spirit flavored with aniseed, which has a taste similar to liquorice. A clear spirit, it is usually drunk diluted with water, which turns it a milky yellow as the water comes into contact with the oils of the aniseed. Pastis has replaced absinthe, the popular Bohemian drink of the 1890s which is now outlawed in most countries as it contains the harmful oil of wormwood. Two of the best known brands are Pernod and Ricard. In Greece the

national drink is *ouzo*, a similarly flavored drink, made from a brandy base. The Spanish version of pastis is called OJEN, and in Turkey, it is RAKI, made from a distilled raisin base. Raki means "lion's milk," and the drink is so called because of its "encouraging" effect and its milky appearance when diluted with water.

TEQUILA is distilled in the Jalisco district of Mexico from pulque, the fermented sap of the maguey, a desert cactus plant also known as the blue agave. The Spanish conquistadores found the Aztecs distilling this spirit when they arrived in Mexico. As in the case of the Persian concubine who is said to have first come across wine, legend has it that it was again a woman, Mayahuetl, who discovered pulque naturally fermenting in the desert. She shared her finding with her husband Patecatl, who then began to ferment it on a regular basis for the gods, priests and warriors. The maguey plant takes eight to ten years to mature. The heart of the plant is known as the piña, as it resembles a pineapple; it weighs anything from 80 pounds

to 175 pounds. These are first cooked, then mashed to extract the juice. This is then fermented for about two days and distilled in a pot still at a low proof (106° US). Most of the distillate is not aged but bottled at once, but a small portion is matured in wood and labeled *añejo* (aged).

The traditional way to drink tequila is as follows: lick the hollow between your thumb and forefinger and lightly sprinkle salt on the area; lick the salt; take a gulp of tequila; then suck a wedge of lime (or, in a pinch, lemon) . . . repeat!

The best known tequila cocktails are the Margarita and the Sangrita (diminutive of blood), something like a Bloody Mary (see recipe section).

BITTERS

Bitters are spirits flavored with herbs and roots of medicinal nature like the original concoctions of the medical apothecaries before they decided to sweeten their products. Today there are two types: those used to flavor and color mixed drinks; and those which are drunk, usually diluted, as an *aperitif* or *digestif*.

Of the first type, Angostura bitters is the most famous. Originally Angostura was a medicine concocted by a Dr. Johann Gotlieb Benjamin Siegert, a German army surgeon who joined Simon Bolivar's army during the Venezuelan War of Independence. Dr. Siegert had embarked upon a study of equatorial diseases and the medicine developed from his attempt to see what effect the local herbs had on these fevers. Soon his secret recipe was in demand far and wide, and in 1850 he gave up his medical practice and set up in business exporting his bitters. The firm moved from Venezuela to Trinidad where Angostura bitters are produced today. Angostura bitters have a long-standing association with the British Royal Navy where they are used as a flavoring to gin in what is called pink gin, because of the color a few drops of the dark liquid give it. They are also used in many other mixed drinks and are a must for any home bar. So, too, in the kitchen where they are handy for flavoring soups, gravies and stews.

Other flavoring bitters are Law's peach bitters and orange bitters, both produced in England.

Of the second type of bitters—the kind which are usually drunk diluted as an *aperitif* or *digestif* because of the medicinal herbs which flavor them—there are quite a number:

AMER PICON is a brandy-based bitters made in France which is flavored with quinine, orange peel and other herbs. It is usually drunk diluted with water and ice, and a dash of grenadine to sweeten it.

CAMPARI is an Italian bitters, very popular at home and abroad. In Italy it is also marketed ready mixed with soda in small bottles. Besides being drunk with soda, it also makes a delicious drink called Americano (see recipe section).

FERNET BRANCA is another Italian bitters, a very bitter one indeed, recommended if you are feeling queasy.

UNDERBERG is the German equivalent, strong and bitter, recommended as "the hair of the dog that bit you" for the morning after.

UNICUM is a bitters made in Italy, rather more syrupy than

Campari. The Italians are great drinkers of bitters which they find helpful in alleviating the national disease *mal di fegato*, liver trouble. They have even made one based on artichokes called CYNAR, which has such an original taste that many uninitiated find it hard to conquer.

RECIPES

MARGARITA
1½ tequila
½ Cointreau
1 lime juice
Shake and strain into a glass, the rim of which has been coated with salt.

SANGRITA
1½ tequila
3 tomato juice
1 tbs. lemon juice
Juice of 1 onion
Dash of chile sauce
Mix in a tall glass with ice.

AMERICANO
1 Campari
2 sweet vermouth
Serve in a tumbler with ice and top with soda water.

NEGRONI
1 Campari
1 sweet vermouth
2 gin
Serve in a tumbler with ice and top with soda water. (The Negroni was invented by Count Negroni at Giacosa's in Florence as an embellishment of the Americano.)

GLOSSARY

APERITIF: the French word for a drink taken before meals to stimulate the appetite.

APPLEJACK: the American name for apple brandy. Originally it was made by leaving a pail of cider out overnight to freeze, then skimming off the ice (which represented the water content) and collecting the unfrozen alcohol.

AQUA VITAE: the Latin name for a distilled spirit, meaning "the water of life."

BONNE CHAUFFE: the second distillate in cognac production.

BROUILLIS: the first distillate in cognac production.

BOOTLEGGER: illegal seller of liquor, who has not paid excise tax.

CARAMEL: burnt sugar used in minute quantities to color spirits.

CHARRING: the slight burning of the inside of a wooden cask in which spirits are to be stored and/or matured.

CHAIS: ground-level storage room in which cognac is matured.

COFFEY STILL: a spirit still developed by Aeneas Coffey in the 1830s for the continuous distillation of spirits. Also known as the patent still, continuous still, or column still.

CONGENERS: organic compounds produced in addition to ethyl alcohol during fermentation and distillation, and developed during the aging of spirits in wood.

CONTINUOUS STILL: see COFFEY STILL.

DIASTASE: an enzyme produced by germinating cereals; it converts starch molecules into sugar.

DIGESTIF: the French term for a drink usually taken after a meal to aid digestion.

DRAFF: Vegetable residue from the mashing of cereals in the production of Scotch whisky; it is used for cattle fodder.

DRAM: colloquial term used in Scotland for a shot of whisky.

ELIXIR: an imaginary liquid which the alchemists believed would transform base metals into gold; the quintessence of a spirit.

ENZYME: an organic catalyst which brings about a chemical reaction in another substance without itself being changed in the process.

ESTERS: organic chemical compounds largely responsible for the flavor in spirits.

FEINTS: that part of the distillate which contains too many impurities and which in the process of distillation is segregated from the middle run and redistilled with the next batch of liquor.

FERMENTATION: the decomposition of sugar by yeast into ethyl alcohol and carbon dioxide.

FUSEL OIL: a general term for the higher alcohols present in the distilled spirits.

GAY-LUSSAC: the continental European system for determining the alcoholic content of a beverage, invented in the early nineteenth century by Joseph Gay-Lussac.

LOW WINES: the first distillate in the production of Scotch whisky.

MADILLA: a term used in the rum trade for the middle of the run, or "good heart" of the spirit.

MASH: grain which has been steeped in hot water to moisten the starch, a necessary preparation for the fermentation process.

MALT: Grain, usually barley, which has been allowed to germinate and is then frustrated.

MEAD: an alcoholic beverage made from honey.

MUST: the unfermented juice of the grape.

PATENT STILL: see COFFEY STILL.

PHYLLOXERA: a parasitic disease of the grape vine.

POMACE: the cake of pulped grapes or other fruit left over after the juice has been pressed out.

PUB: abbreviation for "public house," the standard English drinking establishment.

SPEAK-EASY: Clandestine drinking establishment rampant during Prohibition in the United States, where one had to whisper a password to be admitted.

WASH: the brew which has been fermented from the worts in the production of Scotch whisky; it is this which is actually distilled.

WORTS: the liquid drawn off from the mash of grain in the production of Scotch whisky; it is this which is fermented.

ALCOHOLIC STRENGTH

°Gay Lussac	Proof (American)	Proof (British, or Sykes)
44	88	77.00
45	90	78.75
46	92	80.50
47	94	82.25
48	96	84.00
49	98	85.75
50	100	87.50
57.14	114.28	100.00
60	120	105.00
70	140	122.50
80	160	140.00
90	180	157.50
100	200	175.00

INDEX